Head to Tail Wellness

Western Veterinary Medicine
Meets Eastern Wisdom

Stacy Fuchino, V.M.D.

WILEY

Wiley Publishing, Inc.

Howell Book House
An imprint of Turner Publishing Company
www.turnerbookstore.com

For general information on our other products and services or to obtain technical support please contact our Customer Care Department within the U.S. at (877) 762-2974, outside the U.S. at (317) 572-3993 or fax (317) 572-4002.

Wiley also publishes its books in a variety of electronic formats. Some content that appears in print may not be available in electronic books. For more information about Wiley products, please visit our web site at www.wiley.com.

Library of Congress Cataloging-in-Publication data is available from the publisher upon request.

ISBN: 978-0-470-50612-7

Printed in the United States of America

10 9 8 7 6 5 4 3 2

Illustrations by Jeremy Mooney
Book design by Lissa Auciello-Brogan
Book production by Wiley Publishing, Inc. Composition Services

Contents

Chapter 8

Chapter 9

Chapter 10

Chapter 11

Acknowledgments

Thanks to Laura, the supporter of all my endeavors, no matter how far I reach for the stars. Thanks to my sons, Hayden and Cooper ("Coop"), for their patience while their dad played author. Also thanks to the pets, Cali, Davis, Rey, Dante, Happa, Sheba, and Hannah, who were the inspiration for me to investigate total wellness for pets. A big thank you goes to Geovanni, who enabled me to put my ideas together and make this book a reality; also a big thank you to Jeff for his contribution towards this book, and to all others, both humans and pets, who have contributed in their own way. I owe a huge thanks to Brandon, who helped me immensely in organizing the book and accomplishing my vision. Lastly, thanks to Wiley for taking on a subject that is essential: improving the bond between people and their pets.

About the Author

Known to his loyal clients as Dr. Stacy, Stacy Fuchino, V.M.D., received his veterinary degree from the prestigious University of Pennsylvania School of Veterinary Medicine, then completed an externship at New York City's renowned 24-Hour Animal Medical Center. After the externship, he engaged in a year of intense studies at the California Animal Hospital under world-acclaimed veterinarian Dr. Stephen Ettinger. Subsequently, Dr. Stacy went into private practice in Los Angeles and elected to augment his training by pursuing studies in traditional Eastern medicine at the Chi Institute for Animals and in

feng shui at the American Feng Shui Institute. At his state-of-the-art Palos Verdes Pet Hospital in Redondo Beach, California, he has treated animals suffering from nearly every ailment that can affect a pet: arthritis, allergies, kidney disease, heart and lung problems, cancer, behavioral problems, skin conditions, and many more. He blends a wide array of veterinary services, including surgery, X-rays, and blood tests with acupuncture and herbal remedies. Dr. Stacy has made numerous television appearances. He is currently involved with the longest-running cat series on television, "Housecat Housecall," as a consulting producer. He and his wife, Laura, have two children and three Jack Russell Terriers.

Introduction

In my work as a veterinarian, I combine Western diagnostic and treatment methods with Eastern healing principles. When potential clients hear about my work, the first question they usually ask is: "Why should I bother to learn about a different approach to my pet's health than the one I'm already familiar with—the one my parents grew up with?" I have heard many variations on this "why" question during early meetings with pet owners about the health of their dog, cat, bird, or other beloved animal. Over the years, I've found that regardless of the animal I'm trying to treat and regardless of the pet owner's past experiences, the best answer to this question usually involves a story about some pet I've helped in the past. Because many of the pet owners I work with are focused on the health and well-being of a single animal, that household scenario is a common element to most of the case studies I will be sharing with you in this book. You will notice that the majority of these stories focus on the general population of the pets we see in my office, mainly dogs and cats. My treatments have also extended to small mammals and birds, and to larger animals, such as horses. Most of these stories are beyond the scope of this book.

Gussie

Jane was a 72-year-old retiree who had lost her husband about ten years before I met her. Because she was no longer close to either of her children, Jane's current companion in life was Gussie, a Scottish Terrier, who had helped fill the void after her husband's passing. Jane had owned Gussie for six years and he was really all she had left in life.

When Gussie became more and more lethargic, a friend's strong recommendation led Jane to bring Gussie to my office for an examination.

1

Pets of all ages and species benefit from head to tail wellness.

Jane was skeptical that anything I had to offer would work, but she felt she had no other option. With some of the people who come to see me, their pets are in such bad health that they're willing to try just about anything, including a visit to a veterinarian who uses Eastern healing principles. This attitude presents a challenge, though, because the animal inevitably picks up a lot of energy (both good and bad) from the owner. If the pet owner is reluctant to let the treatment work, then it's not going to work very well. In this case, Jane was willing to give my treatment a chance . . . and so was Gussie.

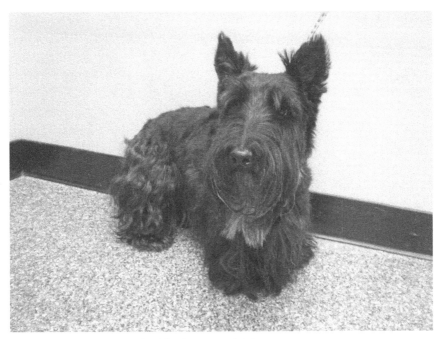

Gussie now enjoys everyday life despite arthritis.

I engaged in a long discussion with Jane about Gussie's history, eating habits, and current condition. I examined the home environment personally. I learned that Jane and Gussie had enjoyed an active, engaged relationship in the early years, but problems had recently developed as their lifestyle had grown much more sedentary. Gussie was severely overweight. He had once been an upbeat, vibrant presence in Jane's life, but now he would simply lie in the bedroom for hours on end until Jane physically moved him. Shortly after meeting Jane and Gussie, I could tell that they were each getting on in years, but that they still had the possibility of enjoying a good quality of life together. The key to revitalizing the relationship, and restoring them both, lay in looking not only at Gussie's symptoms, but also at the larger relationship between Jane and Gussie and the energy (called *chi*, which I'll discuss in chapter 2, "Evaluating Pet Wellness through Purposeful Petting") that passed between them.

After conducting a full examination of Gussie that included bloodwork, blood pressure analysis, an EKG, and X-rays, I explained to Jane that I was just as interested in restoring her dog's health as she was. That helped to build a bond between us, because even though Jane was skeptical, she was deeply concerned about her dog. Then I told her the bad news: Gussie had arthritis in his lower back and was very nearly paralyzed. The good news was that, so far, I had a perfect record when it came to healing paralyzed dogs. Now she was interested!

I told Jane that I needed her help. Gussie could get better—but only if she and I worked together as partners. The pattern of interaction, the flow of energy (*chi*) between her and Gussie, would have to change. The *relationship* would have to change. If Jane was willing to adjust their lifestyle and make some changes in the way she and Gussie approached the day, then I was confident that we could win this battle. If she wasn't willing to change the way she connected with Gussie, then the battle was already over. That, too, got her attention. Together, we undertook a plan to change the way the two interacted.

Jane changed her daily routine with Gussie. Whereas she previously wasn't even willing to walk Gussie on a regular basis, she now made her interactions with him one of the high points of their day, and she got him walking again. Jane began to show confidence in Gussie's ability to get better, thereby sending more positive energy his way. And she became more aware of her pet's feedback to her. She also helped me implement a series of treatments with Eastern herbs designed to improve Gussie's energy flow. And, with some help and guidance from me, she changed his diet.

Within two weeks of this treatment plan, Gussie was walking better on his own initiative—and soon he was living an active, healthy lifestyle. What was just as satisfying to me was to see that *Jane's* condition had improved. She was sharper, more alert, more alive, and more mobile. We were able to add five quality years of life to that relationship by changing the flow of energy between Jane and Gussie.

Initially, Jane had been very skeptical, even downright negative, to the idea of using Eastern medicine to complement Western veterinary medicine. She decided to give it a try, though, and the results we achieved together more than justified her open-mindedness.

Roscoe

I met Mike, a construction worker, at a party. We began chatting, and I mentioned that I was a veterinarian. I soon learned that Mike, like

Roscoe as he started to show the effects of aging.

Jane, was a pet owner whose relationship to his pet was deeply important to him. He told me that he and his dog, Roscoe, had "been through everything" together; in fact, Mike felt he was closer to Roscoe than he was to most members of his own family.

Unfortunately, Roscoe had serious issues with arthritis and a major lower-back problem. When I mentioned to Mike that I had a good record of helping dogs in Roscoe's situation with a combination of dietary changes and acupuncture, his expression instantly changed. The conversation, which had been free-flowing and pleasant, suddenly stopped short.

"That stuff doesn't work," he said. "I know for a fact it doesn't work, so don't try to get me to do it."

Despite his obvious discomfort, I asked Mike a few more questions and soon learned that he had spent nearly $1,000 on acupuncture treatments for Roscoe—and had gotten no positive results.

This told me two important things. First and foremost, it told me that Mike was deeply committed to his pet's health, which was very important. Second, it told me that he had run into someone who claimed to have proficiency in acupuncture, but probably didn't.

After a moment or so, I looked Mike in the eyes and said, slowly but firmly, "If you bring Roscoe to my office, I guarantee that I can improve his condition."

There was a long silence. Then Mike told me he'd think about it.

For a long time after that conversation, I wondered why I'd said what I had. As a veterinarian, I can't really *guarantee* any outcome, positive or negative. But something told me to say the word *guarantee* in this case, and now I'm very glad I did. Not long after our initial meeting, Mike brought Roscoe in for his first examination. Within one day of receiving the first course of a basic acupuncture treatment, the dog had regained 50 percent of his mobility and was well on his way to regaining more in the coming weeks.

Mike was surprised, but ecstatic. At one point he said to me, "I actually have to start believing in this stuff now!"

Bippy

Doris was a breeder of Wire Fox Terriers. In fact, she was one of the most successful breeders in the country within that specialty. One of her dogs was pregnant and needed a cesarean section, so Doris asked me to perform the procedure.

Because she was a professional at the peak of her career as a top breeder, Doris often found herself investing between $5,000 and $10,000 in one of her dogs. (This included costs related to breeding, care, and competing in dog shows.) By necessity, she'd come to adopt a rigid, hard-nosed, bottom line–driven way of looking at the animals under her care. I think that's one of the reasons that what happened during the cesarean was so remarkable to her.

One of the newborn pups was unresponsive. I checked its pulse and breathing and found that both were nonexistent. Immediately, I began an acupuncture procedure on the little pup, though I knew that Doris didn't expect me to do it. I knew, too, that she was not likely to be eager for me to find a way to save a "runt" who might well end up being given away. But something told me to do it anyway. Perhaps Doris didn't object too much because she didn't think I'd actually be able to accomplish anything with this deeply distressed animal.

Fortunately, the acupuncture worked, and the puppy responded in a matter of minutes and began suckling. The story gets even better: Bippy, the new pup, became a great dog for Doris's kennel! Doris, who had been a naysayer when it came to Eastern treatment methodologies, was now a believer.

A suffering dog gets another chance at life after acupuncture treatment.

Tabitha

Eleanor, a graphic artist, was in love with her tabby cat, Tabitha, but in recent weeks the two had run into some big problems. When Eleanor tried to pet Tabitha, the cat went into a seizure. The seizures seemed to be caused by Eleanor's physical contact with Tabitha! These episodes were quite frightening for both Eleanor and Tabitha because Tabitha often became quite aggressive during the disorientation from the seizures and would even lunge at Tabitha and bite her.

A local veterinarian told Eleanor that he wanted to give her cat some drugs to control the seizures, but this approach didn't seem quite right to Eleanor. The seizures seemed to have been caused by touch. Was simply giving her cat drugs going to solve the underlying problem? The veterinarian dismissed Eleanor's questions and insisted on his "standard" line of treatment. Eleanor said she wanted to do a little research on her own.

When she asked her doctor whether acupuncture might help Tabitha, the doctor's response was brisk: "If you change the treatment to include acupuncture, it won't help your cat, and may kill her."

Fewer seizures means more fun for Tabitha.

Following her instincts, Eleanor decided to ignore the doctor's warning—even though he made her sign a waiver acknowledging that he was no longer responsible for the cat's health or the outcome of her care. She came to me and we began a series of acupuncture treatments. Within a week, we were able to reduce the number of seizures by 75 percent. They are now a once-a-week occurrence rather than a daily occurrence.

Far from killing the cat, the acupuncture treatment, combined with changes in Tabitha's nutrition and environment, dramatically improved her quality of life—and helped to restore a pattern of love and intimacy between pet and owner.

What Made These Pets' Recoveries Possible?

Pet owners who are used to looking at medicine—and just about everything else—through a Western lens often ask me about the "technique" that made such turnarounds possible. Was it "just" acupuncture or "just" dietary change that did the trick? Actually, no single Eastern healing therapy was the single "reason" for any of these dramatic changes. What made the difference was a willingness to consider everything (a *holistic* method)—the symptoms, the animal, the pet owner, and the environment shared by both—as part of a single process, and then act sensitively and appropriately in a way that is likely to restore the health of the entire system. Western medicine—which is much more likely to identify isolated "problems" that are looked at individually, without regard to the animal's overall well-being—has yet to integrate this holistic approach.

Sometimes pet owners hear accounts like the ones I've just shared with you and are more than a little skeptical that what I'm describing could actually take place. They wonder if I'm some kind of modern-day medicine salesman, making up stories of miraculous cures that can't possibly be legitimate, or exaggerating my claims for my own sake. Let me assure you that the medical particulars of the cases I've shared with you are accurate—though of course I've changed people's names and a few other identifying details in order to respect their privacy. But what you've just read *is* clinically accurate, and it is the tip of the iceberg. There are dozens, even hundreds, of cases where people's pets have experienced similarly dramatic turnarounds as a result of this kind of treatment.

In other cases, the reaction I get from people is exactly the opposite. Sometimes pet owners hear stories like the ones I've just shared with you, and they assume that there must be something magical in what I do, something otherworldly, strange, or unexplainable. Some people even start talking about miracles!

Both of these reactions— "you must be exaggerating or lying" and "you must be a miracle worker"—are off base and they both miss something important: It is the *combination* of Western veterinary science and Eastern healing methods that makes these remarkable recoveries possible. Once people understand this assimilation, they begin to understand what actually took place in these cases. They begin to see that what the pet owners and I accomplished was neither trickery nor any kind of miracle. What we did was, instead, something much more down-to-earth and pragmatic: *We used what actually works from* **both** *traditions*. For instance, before treating Gussie, I did a standard examination incorporating all the appropriate Western diagnostic tools; after using acupuncture to revive Bippy, I did a routine analysis of her blood pressure and other vital signs, using the conventional procedures I had mastered in veterinary school.

Integrating Eastern and Western Medicine

It's certainly not accurate to say that I "reject" Western veterinary medicine, although you hear some people talk in those terms when it comes to animal care. I'm not one of those people. I could hardly reject "standard" medical science. After all, I'm a trained practitioner, and I like to use what works! My background includes:

- A degree from the University of Pennsylvania Veterinary School

- An internship in Medicine and Surgery under world-renowned veterinarian Dr. Steve Ettinger

- Training and certification in Traditional Chinese Veterinary Medicine, including practicing Eastern and Western methods in animal care for over a decade

- Published articles on the blending of Eastern and Western medical care in pets

- Active in the research and development of nutritional supplements for pets that take advantage of what I've learned from both the Eastern and Western traditions.

What I want you to understand about my work with animals is that I *take the best elements* from Eastern *and* Western traditions and combine these elements to help pets (and their owners) improve their quality of life. Once you understand this point, I think you'll begin to see why the principles I'm explaining in this book are important.

Let me share with you, in broad terms, exactly what each of these two rich medical traditions offers to pets and to the people who love and care for them.

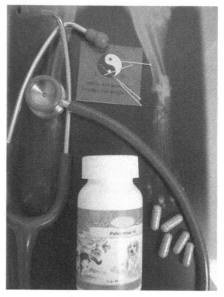

Conventional Western veterinary medicine meets traditional Eastern therapies.

Western Medical Methods

Western medicine has, over the years, developed a remarkably effective set of tools and systems for *diagnosing specific problems*. If you think of the television dramas about doctors and medicine that have been popular in the United States in recent years, you'll see exactly what I mean. The series *House M.D.* is basically a detective show with a single answer waiting to be discovered. It's a mystery story that offers up a series of symptoms—some clear, some ambiguous, some misleading—that doctors must identify, sometimes using very sophisticated equipment. The show essentially challenges the doctors—the "detectives"—to solve the mystery by logically connecting the relevant symptoms to a particular disorder, or perhaps even a series of disorders. Once that difficult work is done and a treatment is administered, the "detective" can consider the case closed.

This approach to medicine, where the symptoms are correctly identified and linked to a provable diagnosis, has achieved astonishing things, and it would be foolish to reject this methodology.

If my pet has a malignant tumor—or if I do, for that matter—I definitely want access to the best available tools for spotting the clues that will allow the "detective" working on my behalf to identify, locate, and apprehend the "criminal" (the disease).

All the same, there are clear limitations to the Western approach. Consider the following questions:

- Is the case really closed once the doctor has identified the symptom and used it to identify a particular disease or disorder?

- Has the doctor learned everything that matters about the patient?

- Does the doctor know why the problem *arose* in the first place, and whether other processes of body/mind may be involved?

Very often, Western medicine, for all its undeniable achievements, gets a little distracted by symptoms. That's not a bad thing; it's just an inevitable consequence of the Western method—something we have to understand and, perhaps, compensate for. The Western approach doesn't always treat the whole organism or take into account how the various parts of the organism are connected, or ask how the organism interacts with its environment. In many cases, Western medicine ends up treating only segments of the body when a more comprehensive approach is in order. And this is where the principles of Eastern medicine—principles that have been generating astonishing results of their own for thousands of years—come into play.

Eastern Medical Methods

To complement the important and essential *symptom-focused* questions of Western medicine, the Eastern tradition asks additional *process-focused* questions:

- How are body/mind processes connected to each other?
- What are the relationships between these systems, and are those relationships in balance?
- How is the environment affecting this patient?
- What is this patient's condition as a whole?
- What is the patient's energy flow telling you?

These questions, too, are important. They are the kinds of questions I used to treat the pets I told you about earlier. Without questions like these, I believe those animals would have suffered needlessly and died early. All too often, these questions are marginalized or completely overlooked in Western veterinary practice. For instance, the number of veterinarians who ask questions about the specifics of the relationship between pet and

This symbol represents the yin and yang balance that is needed in mind, body, and environment for your pet.

owner, or about the physical environment that the pet shares with the owner, is still very small.

Attitudes Toward Eastern Healing

Now, it is certainly true that modern Western diagnostic tools identify specific health problems in animals that traditional Eastern practitioners, using only the ancient tools, would not be able to spot. Yet it's also true that Eastern therapeutic approaches, which have finally begun to enter the mainstream in the treatment of human patients, are still considered something of a joke by both veterinarians and pet owners. Recall the veterinarian who assured Eleanor that acupuncture would kill her cat; recall Jane's initial dismissal of the entire Eastern healing tradition. These attitudes are common. I believe they reflect a tragic cultural oversight—one that is costing animals, and humans, a price they simply should not have to pay.

I want to be very clear here. This skepticism toward *any* application of Eastern therapies for our pets represents a major quality-of-life issue for both animals *and* humans. Why? Because the link between pet ownership and improved health and well-being in humans has been established beyond any doubt—and Eastern medicine represents an important tool in extending pet life and improving the quality of a pet's life. To put it bluntly, ignoring the most effective treatments for our pets reduces the quality and duration of *our* lives. Our lives, and our life cycles, are linked with those of our pets.

That claim may seem broad, but I assure you that it isn't. Of course, this is not an academic book, and my aim is not to burden you with lots of footnotes and citations. As we begin, though, I do want to share just one relevant quote from the world of human/animal research in order to establish, before we go any further, two absolutely essential points:

1. Your own health is affected by your relationship with your pet.
2. If you ignore the best-possible care for your pet, then you run the risk of damaging your own health.

In our study of 92 white patients who had been admitted to a large university hospital, only 3 of the 53 pet owners died within the first year of admission, while 11 of the 39 people who did not own pets died in the same period. . . . The effect of pet ownership was not present only in people who were socially isolated. It was independent of marital status and access to social support from other people. . . . Abundant evidence suggests that the companionship provided by a pet can both reduce the frequency of serious disease and prolong life.

—From the chapter "Health Consequences of Pet Ownership" in the book Pet Loss and Human Bereavement, by Erika Friedmann, Aaron A. Katcher, Sue A. Thomas, and James J. Lynch (Wiley-Blackwell, 1991)

Symbiosis

Another important concept that relates to the relationship between pets and owners is *symbiosis*. Symbiosis is the mutually beneficial association of two different organisms.

Symbiosis is shown here where the soil and plants thrive with one another's interrelationship.

I believe our relationships with our pets are important *because* these relationships are symbiotic. Our lives are interconnected with the lives of our pets, and that interconnectedness supports both humans and animals.

Our relationships with our pets are not trivial, any more than our relationships with our family members or with the earth that sustains us or with the larger universe are trivial. Our relationships with our pets *matter*. These relationships are both enduring and significant, and they benefit us in ways that we do not always understand, but that have profound effects on our lives as we actually live them. Once they enter our lives, our pets are dependent on us, but in a very real sense we need them, too—in ways that are undeniable and worth recognizing. Jane definitely needed Gussie. Mike definitely needed Roscoe. Doris didn't believe she would ever need Bippy, but she did! And Eleanor definitely needed Tabitha.

Some people who don't have pets are surprised to learn what pet owners have learned: Pets become some of our best teachers in life. As we watch their life cycles unfold, we can learn a great deal about the passages we navigate in our own lives.

Three Reasons I Wrote This Book

This much is certain: We are linked to our pets in a way that Western medicine has been able to identify, but not, perhaps, to explain properly. One reason I wrote this book is because I believe it is time for people to consider *why* this extraordinary link exists. I'll share my own answer to that question in chapter 1, "The Yin and Yang of Pet Care." It has to do with something called *chi* (pronounced "chee"), or vital energy.

Another reason I wrote this book is because I believe by using a variety of techniques to complement Western approaches and manipulate the vital energy, the *chi* that flows through us and our pets, we can improve our pets' quality of life—and do a better job of caring for ourselves *and* our pets as connected entities. If we do that, we can actually prevent many illnesses from arising in the first place!

Today, questions of balance, energy flow, human/pet interaction, and response to environment often don't even enter into the discussions veterinarians have with pet owners. My final reason for writing this book is the hope of changing and thereby improving the quality of the dialogue we have with the people who care for our pets.

Before We Move On . . .

Let me share one more important point with you. I started my career as a veterinarian who trusted Western techniques implicitly, and relied on those techniques to resolve each and every problem I encountered.

I only started focusing on Eastern medicine in my practice because I "hit a wall." I realized that too many pets had chronic problems that stubbornly evaded diagnosis by veterinarians trained in Western techniques. I realized that in these situations, conventional veterinary approaches had little or nothing to offer animals with chronic diseases such as arthritis, renal failure, liver failure, or cancer. I felt strongly—and still feel strongly—that adopting a holistic approach, and treating pets as part of the larger living environment, gave me the opportunity to extend the span of these animals' lives, while at the same time improving the quality of their lives. By combining both Eastern and Western approaches, I was able to help them live with their condition and sustain a quality of life that had seemed impossible to many pet owners.

I have been able to help animal patients that other veterinarians were not able to help because I've been able to add new methods to their treatment—not because I've abandoned Western medicine. To the contrary, I take full advantage of Western scientific advances, procedures, and diagnostics at every possible opportunity and I urge pet owners to do the same! What I have found, however, is that by using Eastern principles that are proven to be clinically effective to *complement and enhance* the more familiar Western treatment regimens, I stand a much better chance of helping the pets, and the owners, who are depending on me for care.

These principles also have the advantage of being considerably less expensive, over the long term, than relying exclusively on Western approaches. To learn more about these Eastern ideas of medicine (and life) that transformed my own practice . . . and the lives of so many of my patients . . . read on.

Chapter 1

The *Yin* and *Yang* of Pet Care

Human beings are born [because of] the accumulation of Chi. When it accumulates there is life. When it dissipates there is death. . . . There is one Chi that connects and pervades everything in the world. . . . The highest Yin is the most restrained. The highest Yang is the most exuberant. The restrained comes forth from Heaven. The exuberant issues forth from Earth. The two intertwine and penetrate forming a harmony, and [thus] things are born.

—Zhuangzi, 4th century B.C.

Zhuangzi, an ancient Chinese philosopher, connected the vital energy known as *chi* to the elemental creative forces of the universe. He saw *yin* as the yielding or feminine universal force, *yang* as the exuberant or male universal force, and *chi* as the pervasive, healing, and animating energy that makes life itself possible *within* that universe. Whether or not you consider it "Western" or "Eastern," Zhuangzi's sketch of the universe remains useful even thousands of years later. It is a pragmatic, reality-based way to address questions of health and wellness. It is not the only way to address those questions, of course, but it is *one* way of addressing them, and it has delivered extraordinarily positive results to people and animals for a very long time.

Many people wonder: What do Zhuangzi's ideas really have to offer me and my pet? The answer is *balance*.

When you look at the classic yin-yang symbol shown here, you can see it: balance, movement, interdependence, and interconnection. If you look carefully, you may also see in this timeless symbol an intriguing alternative to some familiar notions of a stagnant, fixed existence. Michelangelo painted God as an old man with a beard who reclined majestically, a king who towered physically above His creation. Eastern thought envisions something very different: an intertwining divine *process*.

Zhuangzi, along with many other great Eastern thinkers, calls your attention to a process of continuous universal creativity. This is a process in which *harmony* is the most sublime outcome, a process in which the life force that animates human beings is the same force that enlivens a plant, a river—and, yes, a pet such as a dog, a cat, or a horse. *Yin* and *yang* are what make that process possible. You have probably seen the yin-yang symbol on jewelry, on food products, in books, and in a thousand other places, but you likely do not always ask yourself: What does the symbol really *mean*? Is it a fad, a trademark,

The yin-yang symbol represents balance, movement, interdependence, and interconnection.

The Characteristics of *Yin* and *Yang*

Yin is traditionally identified with . . .

- "Inside-ness" (for example, internal organs)
- Night
- Cold
- Deficiency
- Chronic conditions
- Reduced stature
- Moistness
- Rest

Yang is traditionally identified with . . .

- "Outside-ness" (for example, skin)
- Day
- Heat
- Excess
- Acute conditions
- Expanded stature
- Dryness
- Activity

or a shrewd piece of corporate branding? Actually, it is an ancient symbol of harmony and balance. The round shape of the symbol represents the globe and the larger universe. *Yin*—the dark component—contains an element of light. *Yang*—the light component—contains an element of darkness. Together, they describe the opposing, complementary qualities in natural phenomena.

The yin-yang symbol reminds you that all things are constantly in motion, and that there needs to be a balance in everything that evolves and cycles in your life. Everyday experience gives you plenty of examples of these cycles: night follows day, activity follows rest, leisure follows productivity. These phenomena follow each other in sequence. In other words, without one, the other cannot take place. The *interaction* of the *yin* and *yang* is what brings the living world into being.

In Eastern philosophy, there is no designation of which is "supposed to" come first, *yin* or *yang*. The real question is how *yin* and *yang* **relate to each other** in order to maintain balance and harmony. You may encounter this question of harmony over and over again during the day, without realizing that it is really *yin* and *yang* playing out in your life. For example: How do you balance work and free time? The more work you do the less free time you have; if you're not careful, your life can fall out of balance. Suppose you overcompensate: You will quickly learn that too much play can also put stress on your life. How can you survive without focusing appropriately on your monetary income? The same potential for harmony—or disharmony—exists in virtually every area of your life: time alone, time with others; consuming calories and burning calories; taking and giving; teaching and learning. As a human being, you attempt to find a balance between these opposites.

Life well lived is not a destination, but a process of finding balance. You can probably think of famous people whose lives have fallen seriously *out* of balance; you can likely also call to mind personal encounters with people who seemed *in* balance, who possessed a deep inner reservoir of purpose, calm, and equilibrium.

What is the source of that harmony? Do you feel it, or live it, or both? In the end, you may find that the best way to "get there" is simply to keep the influences of *yin* and *yang* cycling.

Yin and *yang* are all about balance. They are part of a process. Restoring balance to your life, finding balance with the environment in which you live, aligning yourself and your environment with something larger than yourself, something vast that is already in balance—these are the principles that can improve your pet's quality of life, and your own.

So how do you find this balance? By harnessing *chi*—the universal life force, the pervasive healing energy. The greatest goal of Eastern medicine is to use *chi* to restore balance and harmony to your life. It is not a strange, foreign, or untested principle. To the contrary, it has been "field tested" for thousands of years and has delivered extraordinary results to people, and to animals, in many different cultures and across a huge span of history.

The Power of *Chi*: Case Studies from My Practice

The world has obstacles, and every day you are battling around, over, and through these obstacles. These ongoing battles can cause a strain in a body's system over time. *Chi* helps you—and your pet—to repair the system. This idea of harnessing *chi* to restore balance and wellness is worth a closer look. Let me share a few case studies from my own practice that can give you a clearer picture of the power of *chi*.

Cornflake

Cornflake was an elderly horse who had been having persistent intestinal problems. A friend asked me to take a look at him and share any thoughts I might have about changes that could improve his condition.

Another veterinarian had already seen Cornflake; the drugs he prescribed had done little to improve the chronic intestinal blockages that were making Cornflake's life miserable. None of the drugs seemed to work; the horse's condition had only deteriorated. The only option that the other veterinarian could present at this stage was surgery. As it happened, this other veterinarian had been focusing exclusively on the *disorder* Cornflake had presented: *colic* (persistent abdominal pain). I wanted to take a broader look at the *environment* in which Cornflake

Cornflake's intestinal problems were solved through changes to his diet and his environment.

was living and see the effect that imbalances in his environment were possibly having on his overall state of wellness.

To do that, I asked a different set of questions than the other veterinarian had been asking. Instead of asking, "How do we get rid of the colic?" I had to ask, "Where is this horse spending most of his time, and what is the flow of *chi* in that environment?"

The answer to that question gave me my first clue as to what treatment I was going to recommend. I saw that this elderly horse was spending most of his day in a small, cramped stall. The owners came in to clean the stall every day and had Cornflake exercise minimally during these times. He had little opportunity to move during the course of the average day, and the air in the stall was stale, stagnant, and oppressive. That was not conducive to good *chi* flow because clutter and stagnation impede that flow!

Cornflake's physical surroundings were not meaningless details; they were a critical part of the overall question of balance. (I'll explain this concept, called *feng shui,* in more detail later in this chapter.) The idea of trying to examine or treat the horse without examining or "treating" the physical environment where he was spending most of his time was counterproductive. The fact of the matter was that the circulation of life energy in the tiny space to which this old fellow had been confined was severely restricted, and that restriction was a big part of the problem. *There was no way for me to restore balance to Cornflake's intestinal system without also making some changes to his environment. Chi* was not flowing properly through the environment, which meant that *chi* was not flowing properly through the animal. Eastern medicine holds that no organism can thrive in a static environment. There needs to be a good flow of energy in the environment to support healing and balance, and physical movement is a part of supporting that flow.

The first thing I told the owners to do was to change the environment where Cornflake spent most of his day. We opened things up and got Cornflake into a corral area where he could move around more freely. The owner also started a daily exercise program with him. He was no longer eating in the same tiny space where he was "doing his business." He was moving around; he had newer, high-quality hay; and he was given better, fresher food to eat (food with all the nutrients still intact).

After months of increasing problems with colic, Cornflake made rapid improvement after we made these improvements to his environment.

It was not *merely* the change in diet that made the change in Cornflake's condition possible; my experience is that other veterinarians facing similar conditions have changed a horse's diet, but have not seen the rapid improvement that I saw. There is no one "recipe" for a specific ailment like the one Cornflake was suffering from; what makes the difference is a willingness to look at a unique situation—the animal *and* its environment—and to see the individual parts as elements of a single process that can be restored to harmony. The simple (but seemingly nontraditional) treatment, which involved no surgery and no drugs, solved the problem. It wasn't a miracle—it was the restoration of balance between the animal and his environment. Simply changing the diet was not enough. I had to change the physical space in which the horse spent his day. Questions about *how* this step improved energy flow, or what specifically allows energy to do what it does when the environment changes, are certainly valid, but they are of lesser concern to me as a practitioner than the end results I can help to bring about by channeling this energy more effectively. Perhaps someday a researcher can conduct a clinical study to evaluate the effects of changing the physical environment in such cases.

While he was cramped in his smelly stall, Cornflake had minimal access to the *chi* that would return him to a state of balance. Once we got him out into the fresh air and made some simple changes to his diet, he regained that balance and wellness.

Julio

Malvina's Pug, Julio, was a sweet dog with a weight problem. Actually, Malvina, a reporter in her 30s, had a weight problem, too. Both of them were living a rather sedentary, low-energy lifestyle. It was a shared lifestyle that involved a lot of sitting, since Malvina worked from home. The two just didn't get outdoors much . . . and they didn't circulate much *chi*.

I told Malvina that she needed to change her daily routine with Julio by going out for a lot more walks. I also told her that she needed to make sure that Julio cut back on calories. By focusing on her *relationship* with her dog and not merely on Julio's symptoms, Malvina was able to make some changes in Julio's surroundings.

But that wasn't the only change that occurred. Since Malvina was the one taking Julio for his walks, *she* was getting out for more walks as

The restored movement of *chi* in Julio and his environment has helped Julio and Malvina, his owner, live a more balanced and healthier lifestyle.

well. She was changing her own routine and her own surroundings. It's true enough to say that both of them were getting more exercise. It's also true to say that both Malvina and Julio were benefiting from a daily routine that improved their *chi* flow.

After only a few months, Julio's weight was down—and so was Malvina's. The two were happier, healthier, and more active. Today, they're both doing a better job of controlling their weight. Better circulation of the healing force known as *chi* has been a big part of their shared success.

Mermos

Carol's cat, Mermos, had severe asthma. Instead of simply "treating" the cat during an office visit and making a list of symptoms, I asked to take a look at Mermos's living environment.

Carol lived with Mermos in a one-bedroom condominium. It was small and very cluttered with boxes stacked everywhere. Instead of prescribing drugs to Mermos, I gave Carol a "prescription": Improve the flow of *chi* in the space where Mermos spent virtually all of her time. I asked Carol to work with me to find some simple ways to enhance the flow of life energy in that tiny condo.

First I gave her some ideas about how she could maximize the energy flow in the living space. She moved things around; she cleared out a lot of the clutter; and she even took my advice to remove some carpeting and some drapes that were impeding *chi* flow. It may sound implausible at first, but removing that carpeting and those curtains made it easier for life energy to move more freely within that once-stagnant space.

Within a matter of weeks, Mermos started looking and feeling better. Previously the cat had to use an inhaler daily

A dietary and environmental change helped Mermos better acclimate and keep her asthma under control.

or weekly, but she now needs that inhaler only occasionally. This dramatic improvement in the animal's quality of life (and, by extension, the owner's) was the result of some simple changes in the animal's diet and physical living space. Here, the cycle of yin and yang in the living space had been thrown off so dramatically that it was literally draining energy from the body of the cat. The changes in diet, which included fresher food (and specifically, fresh protein sources), supported a more effective use of Mermos's energy, but I believe the changes in her environment had a more profound effect on removing the stagnation that had been robbing the cat of her life force.

Chi Is All Around You . . . but What Is It?

Chi, the life energy that you need to begin healing yourself and your pet, is all around you, but people often don't take advantage of it. I believe a big part of the reason for this is because we simply don't understand this energy.

When I try to explain *chi* to the pet owners I'm working with, people sometimes start to tune out as though I'm speaking a foreign language. I can talk about energy and balance and healing force, but the pet owner simply doesn't have a point of reference. When I mention that *chi* "flows" through the body, the pet owner might start looking a little more engaged. He or she might ask a question like, "You mean it's like the blood flow in the body?"

Chi is somewhat like blood flow—but bigger than that. *Chi* is literally propelling the blood to flow in the body. This flowing movement can be found in many other processes, not all of which take tangible, physical form. As the three case studies I just shared with you suggest, **simple changes in the environment can have a profound effect on *chi* flow, and thus on overall wellness.** You are probably better off thinking of *chi* as an energy force that the environment either makes easier or makes more difficult for you to access.

Look again at Carol and Mermos's story, earlier. Changing the physical environment in Carol's condo had a huge impact on the flow of *chi* in that living space, and on Mermos's health. This brings us to one of the critical points of this book: Removing clutter is good for your pet's health! Many pet owners in the West are surprised, and a little skeptical, when I tell them that clutter in the home is a major obstacle to a pet's health and well-being. The truth, however, is that clutter is a major obstacle to daily *chi* flow. I've seen the proof of this time and time again. Clutter makes it difficult for the life force to flow freely, and when *chi* doesn't flow freely, pets (and people) don't have access to the energy that will sustain them, invigorate them, and help heal them. Most of the pet owners I meet simply don't realize the impact that cluttered, cramped, or poorly ventilated spaces can have on their pets' quality of life—and their own.

Eventually, though, as in Carol's case, the results persuade people that removing clutter must have *something* to do with improving their pets' health. Even after they see the positive results in their own world, though, many pet owners remain a little puzzled about *chi*. What is it, exactly? That's a fair question—and a difficult one to answer. Western science has yet to measure or quantify *chi* in the way that it has measured or quantified, say, brain waves. Yet *chi* exists all the same.

Over the years, I've developed a number of answers for the people who ask me, "What is *chi*?" Some of them appear below.

Chi Is an Invisible Life Force

The shortest, and probably best, answer to the question "What is *chi*?" is that it is an invisible life force that sustains and supports all beings, and that changes in intensity and effect according to the environment and the being it encounters.

Chi is not something you can measure with a machine. Even so, it is definitely something you can feel and access at any moment. Sit up straight and take a nice, deep breath through your nose, without opening your mouth, and you'll feel what I mean.

Chi Is Vital Energy

Any number of authorities, including Zhuangzi, have described *chi* as *vital energy:* energy that makes activity, and life itself, possible. This energy can be managed by breathing, mental focus, and other disciplines. Attempts to label *chi* with such narrow tags as "life-breath" or "bio-energy" fall short, however, because an individual organism's *chi* can, if properly sustained, extend beyond that organism and into the universe at large. By the same token, an individual organism's *chi* can be degraded (as you have seen) by environmental influences and other factors.

Chi Is Metabolic Flow

Traditional Chinese Medicine holds that the body has natural patterns of metabolic energy—*chi*—that flow in predictable channels. In English, these patterns are called *meridians*. Many illnesses are the result of disruptions, imbalances, or blockages of *chi* in the body; Eastern medical practice emphasizes the restoration of healthy, balanced *chi* flow through these channels by means of changes in the environment, herbal medicines, special diets, massage, acupuncture, acupressure, and other therapies. (Acupuncture uses needles to treat disorders, whereas acupressure uses pressure points.)

The meridians on your pet's body are presented in the figures on the next few pages; the dotted lines represent the meridians. In this case, a dog is used for demonstration.

The meridians govern the highway of organ and circulatory networks within the body; this matrix helps regulate the flow of *chi* throughout the body. Trained practitioners can gain access to the internal circulation of *chi* (and blood) by manipulating various points on these meridians, thus stimulating the release of hormone-like substances called *endorphins* that induce a euphoric state of well-being and help the

Pancreas/spleen meridian.

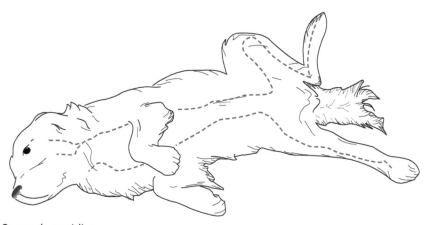

Stomach meridian.

Kidney meridian.

Liver meridian.

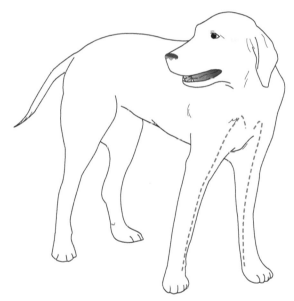

Lungs meridian.

body to cope with discomfort or pain. In fact, some disease states can be detected clinically in animals by stimulating a particular meridian.

In Western medicine's present state of knowledge, much of the "how" behind the use of meridians in acupuncture and acupressure remains a mystery, but we know that they can be used to adjust the balancing functions of the body and thus bring them closer to their optimal levels of functioning.

Large intestine meridian.

Small intestine meridian.

Heart meridian.

Pericardium meridian. (This is the protector of the heart.)

Triple heater meridian. (This is where the chest, abdomen, and pelvis meet. This area regulates metabolism and other bodily fluids and their flow throughout the body.)

Gallbladder meridian.

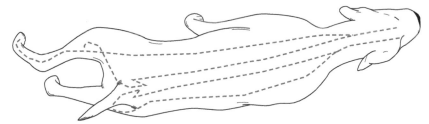

Urinary bladder meridian.

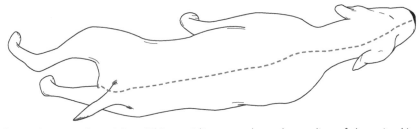

Governing vessel meridian. (This meridian runs along the topline of the animal.)

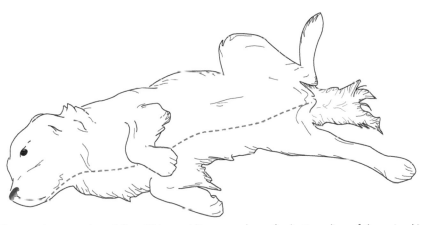

Conception vessel meridian. (This meridian runs along the bottom line of the animal.)

When you use *chi* flow to help animals, you are opening up these channels, which are located all over the body. Often, the reason your pet has a certain ailment is that a certain channel has a problem. And your pet's body, like yours, does a very good job of blocking out areas that are problematic—which sometimes intensifies the problem. The body is simply trying to do what it can to address the blockage or imbalance, but sometimes it needs help in restoring the metabolic flow. If the body doesn't get that help, the result may be stagnation, which can lead to anything from minor problems like aches and pains to major problems like arthritis or a tumor.

Chi Is What You Feel When You Interact Positively with Your Pet

When you've had a long, difficult day at work and you come home and your cat rubs up against you to say hello, that pleasant sensation you feel is due, in part, to *chi* flow. In the Introduction to this book, I shared evidence with you that interactions with pets have a measurable positive effect on human health. I believe that this is due in large measure to the flow of *chi* that people experience when they interact with their pets.

Chi Is What Is in the Natural Environment That Inspires and Awakens You

Let's do a little experiment. I would like you to imagine yourself, just for a moment, in a tiny, cramped, cluttered room where the air is stale and the surroundings are oppressive, chaotic, and stagnant. How do you feel?

Now I'd like you to imagine yourself as you open the door and step outside of that room. You pass through the doorway to find yourself in a big, beautiful garden filled with your favorite flowers or grasses. The weather is beautiful; it's a sunny day, and you feel warm and comfortable. You've got acres of beautiful space to walk around in.

When this sort of thing happens in real life, you feel so much better when you go outside, don't you? The difference in how you feel is due, at least in part, to the enhanced, unblocked *chi* flow in the garden, as compared with the restricted, stagnant levels of *chi* you encountered in that tiny, closed-off room. When you encounter something in the natural environment that inspires and awakens you and you suddenly feel better just by exposing yourself to that environment, the reason is very likely to be a better and larger flow of *chi*.

Maximizing *Chi* Flow

In the end, it really doesn't matter how I describe *chi*. What really matters is how you manage it. Managing *chi*, and maximizing its flow in order to help and support animals, is a big part of my job. This is one of the basic principles I use to do that: **Normally, *chi* flows uninhibited— but *chi* can be *made* inhibited by blockages of various kinds.** As it encounters these blockages, the *chi* is always going to try to flow in the easiest direction. It's going to seek out the points of easiest passage through an organism or an environment. In this way, it's a lot like water.

If there's a large body of water—a river, say—and someone comes along and puts up a dam that obstructs that river, what's going to happen? Well, the water is blocked in one spot, and it's probably going to find a path around the blockage. The area that used to be nourished by the natural flow of that river is no longer going to be nourished by the water. Before too long, the pattern of life there is going to change dramatically. In order to restore the earlier pattern of growth in that area, you have to remove the dam and get the water flowing again through that area.

Chi acts the same way. If you have arthritis or an injury or some other problem, then that problem acts like a dam. There's a roadblock in the body, and the *chi* can no longer flow through that roadblock. As a result, the *chi* is going to go into other areas, probably areas that don't need the help as much as the area with the blockage. **When the bodies of humans or animals experience blockages, the *chi* is not being used as efficiently as possible.** If you know how to channel the *chi*, how to change the environment and the organism so that more of the *chi* reaches the area that was blocked, you're in a position to help the body make the most of *chi*'s healing power.

If *chi* is channeled in the right way, then you and your pet can enjoy years and years of good health. If you don't channel it in the right way, then you and your pet may well end up having health problems.

Feng Shui

The term *feng shui* (pronounced "fung shway") literally translates as "wind-water"—two important vehicles of *chi* in Eastern medicine. *Chi* "rides the wind and scatters, but is retained when encountering water," according to one ancient source.

Feng shui is one of those phrases that people may use a lot without taking the time to understand what they're really saying. If I asked a dozen average Americans what *feng shui* means, I suspect that half a

Quotes to Ponder

*It is more important to know what sort of person has a
disease than to know what sort of disease a person has.*
—Hippocrates (460–377 B.C.)

*No illness which can be treated by the diet should
be treated by any other means.*
—Moses Maimonides (1135–1204)

*The art of healing comes from nature and not
from the physician. Therefore, the physician must start from
nature with an open mind.*
—Paracelsus

dozen would not be able to answer, and the other six might say something about moving furniture around as part of some obscure religious practice. If one person out of the twelve mentioned anything about promoting the healthy flow of *chi,* I'd be very surprised. Some people even think *feng shui* is little more than a fashionable excuse for expensive home redesign projects.

Actually, *feng shui* is the art and science of enhancing *chi* flow by making changes in the physical environment—nothing more than that, and nothing less.

What does this mean to the health of your pet? Well, instead of simply focusing on the animal—the horse who's experiencing colic, for example—we're going to look at the environment in which that animal lives and ask ourselves how effectively *chi* is flowing through that environment. Of course, if you wanted to, you *could* spend a great deal of money, time, attention, and energy completely re-creating a space in order to maximize *chi* flow. In practice, however, you're going to find that some simple and inexpensive changes in the home environment can have dramatic, positive, and rapid effects on the health and well-being of pets and their owners.

Both animals and humans have access to a lot of healing energy. In fact, every living being has access to healing energy. The question is, how much of that energy can you absorb and make use of, and how effectively can you do that?

Personally, I think this is something most people know intuitively. You know you feel better when the cat rubs up against you. You know that the energy flow between you and your pet matters to both of you. And you know, on some level, that what's in your environment is going to affect both you and your pet. These are not outlandish or foreign principles. They're common sense.

In the following chapters, I'll help you put that kind of common sense to work on behalf of you and your pet in simple, practical ways.

But before we move on, I want to leave you with one final thought about *chi* as it relates to your pet's health. In all that follows, you're not going to focus on some isolated *portion* of your pet, and you're not going to focus on your pet *in isolation*. You're going to focus on everything and everyone that *interacts with* your pet, including, but not limited to, the pet's immediate environment and the pet's relationship with you.

Everything your pet interacts with affects her flow of *chi*. To promote that healthy *chi* flow, you're going to make a series of adaptations. As a result, you'll learn to place much more emphasis on relationships, processes, and the flow of energy between you and your pet than on "fixes" for specific, narrowly defined problems. In addition, the promotion of healthy *chi* flow will help both you and your pet to compensate for impurities, pollutants, and stressors that may arise in the environment you share.

Chapter 2

Evaluating Pet Wellness through Purposeful Petting

You and your pet share some obvious things: a common living space, the time you spend together, perhaps a love of the outdoors or a favorite game. You also share other things that may be less obvious: a set of routines that you follow in interacting with one another, an intimacy that is unique to the two of you—and, yes, an effect on one another's energy. This chapter is about *using* all of those things that you share with your pet—the routines, the intimacy, the energy you share—to develop a better ongoing awareness of your pet's wellness.

The emphasis here is on the word *ongoing*. As a pet owner, you want to find ways to notice, and become more and more sensitive to, your pet's health. In fact, the longer you have a relationship with your pet, the more attuned you should be to it, and the more sensitive you should be to your pet's physical well-being. Ideally, your awareness base—the number of things you are capable of noticing about your pet's condition—should expand over time. The ritual I call *purposeful petting* makes that expansion much easier and more enjoyable both for you and for your pet.

A Checklist as a Starting Point

When I began writing this chapter, I wanted to create a simple checklist of all the symptoms and warning signs that a pet owner should be on the lookout for when assessing a pet's condition during purposeful petting. You'll find my best attempt at such a checklist in the following pages. However, while I was creating the checklist, I realized that it had to come with a warning: Once you complete the checklist, do not get so busy that you stop paying attention to your pet's condition.

Purposeful petting is simply petting that notices energy and change. It is not a convenient list of warning signs that you can simply check off once a month—or, even worse, feel guilty about not having checked off at all. Indeed, it is an opportunity to use petting time, or any other period of interaction with your pet, to become more and more aware of what is taking place in your pet's body.

This is petting with a purpose, and it is the opposite of petting distractedly or absentmindedly. My hope is that, by using the checklist that follows as a starting point, you can hone your own intuition about your pet's current state of health and well-being.

Instead of just checking your pet for warning signs of a problem, which sounds too much like a chore, your real goal is to make a point of doing something that you probably already enjoy doing: interact with your pet in a loving way, and notice your pet's condition as you do so. The fact that you're even reading this book suggests that this isn't going to be a particularly difficult item to get onto your to-do list!

You already enjoy loving interactions with your pet. That's the best place to begin. Now, every time you pet or interact with your cat or dog, your goal should be to interact with just a little more conscious observation and a little more awareness than you had last time. Day by day, week by week, month by month, you will become more comfortable with the idea of purposeful petting . . . and you will find that both you and your pet enjoy it a great deal.

You already love connecting with your pet. The trick is to do this with more awareness and more purpose.

Noticing Energy and Change

Purposeful petting is energizing in and of itself, and it's certainly not an "extra" job for you to do. Instead, it's a way of interacting with your pet with the same love, concern, and care you already feel—and with a steadily enlarging circle of awareness for your pet's overall well-being.

If you're a parent, you already have a point of comparison for this kind of purposeful and more-informed interaction. When you give your child a bath, get your child ready for bed, or read your child a story, you probably keep an eye out for things that look or feel different in your child's body, demeanor, and behavior. It's not the kind of thing you do once and then forget about doing until it's time to pay attention again. It's a caring, loving way of connecting with your child.

If you're like most parents, the more you know about raising children, the more adept you are at using interactions with your child to spot changes in your child's physical condition. This is exactly the same kind of awareness I'm suggesting here—only you will be applying that kind of loving attention to your pet.

The Wellness Checklist

Purposeful petting is all about awareness and noticing changes in your pet's physical condition. Following is a list of the kinds of things you should evaluate *each and every time* you pet (or interact in any way with) your cat or dog.

As you interact with your pet, you should notice changes in:

- **Your pet's coat.** It should be free of dander, redness, scabs, parasites, and odor. Was it once shiny and healthy-looking, and is now dull or discolored? Is there missing hair?

- **Your pet's head.** Are there any asymmetries, swollen areas, or other problems? For dogs and cats, are the whiskers broken? The head should be symmetrical, with no protrusions that are irregular in shape. There should be no areas that are painful to the touch, especially when you manipulate the jaw.

- **Your pet's eyes.** Are the whites of the eyes yellowish? Are there changes in the color within the eye? Is there any discharge? Are your pet's eyes clear? Are the whites white, or is there any cloudiness or haziness? Are the pupils symmetrical? The eyelashes should not touch the eyes; the lids should lie comfortably on the eye globe.

- **Your pet's mouth.** Is there any change in color or odor? Does your pet have bad breath that was not a problem before? Are any teeth broken or missing? Are the pet's gums swollen? Is there bleeding in the mouth? The teeth should be white and smooth; the gums should be pink. There should be a thin layer of mucus on the gums and the tongue should be pink with a thin layer of moisture. If the gums are fire-engine red instead of pink, that's a problem.

- **Your pet's ears.** Is there any change in color or odor? Your pet's ears should be free of smell, and there should be a thin oily layer upon touching the inside of the ear. There should be no shaking of the head; there should be no swelling or discoloration of the skin around the ear.

- **Your pet's bone structure.** Does something about your pet's bone structure seem odd or different to you? Is there a change in his gait or stance? Is your pet finding it harder than usual to stand or walk? Are tasks such as walking up stairs more difficult than before? Your pet should walk in a smooth gait; the bones should make no sounds when moving. Your pet should be able to stretch its body structure without obvious hesitation or discomfort. There should be no discomfort during brushing or petting.

- **Your pet's extremities (legs and paws).** Are there any asymmetries, swollen areas, or other unusual conditions? Are they smooth to the touch? Are the nails even with the pads? Are your pet's movements smooth? Is there a limp? Is there a decrease in normal muscle mass? Are there any lumps or bumps?

- **Your pet's eating and drinking patterns.** What eating patterns have been established in your pet's life? How often does your pet normally eat per day? How fast does your pet normally prefer to eat? Where does he eat? Has your pet cut down dramatically on food intake? Has your pet started drinking much more water than usual? To get additional water, does your pet ever search out water from unusual sources, such as a toilet bowl or a pool of standing dirty water?

- **Your pet's pattern of interaction with you and other people.** Is your pet withdrawn and solitary after having been attentive and interested in the past? Does your pet withdraw to solitary spaces, where before he enjoyed your company? Your pet should be bright, alert, and responsive, and should move according to the stimuli that he encounters. Does your pet recognize you as his owner and respond to you? Do you have predictable patterns of play, feeding, and rest?

- **Your pet's awareness of his surroundings.** Your pet probably prefers "indoor" or "outdoor" surroundings. Which is it? How do you know? Your pet has a certain basic "default" level of interest in the events that unfold in his world. How would you rate that level of interest on a scale from one to ten? How would you know if it changed?

- **Your pet's overall energy level.** Was your pet's energy level high and engaged, and is now low and listless? Does your pet look forward to exercise or physical exertion? Does your pet have shortness of breath? What level of activity appears to bring it on? Have you found yourself thinking that your pet seems to be growing older quickly?

EMPTY   FULL

Finally, is anything bothering you about your pet, based on your knowledge and history with this animal? Does something not seem right about your pet's body, general demeanor, or connection with you? *Does his energy seem different?*

Acting on Signs of Imbalance

And now, a word of advice about purposeful petting: **You must *act* on what you notice.** Sometimes pet owners notice important changes in their pets' behavior, physical condition, or energy level . . . and then do not take action on or mention what they notice to their veterinarian.

For both people and animals, balance is the key to a healthy life.

Why is this? Sometimes it's because you tell yourself, "Well, that's just what happens when a pet gets older." For instance, you might notice that a pet is having trouble standing or walking or is *swaybacked* (that is, experiencing curving of the spine), and you might dismiss it as a sign of old age. Believing that every pet eventually gets old, you do not mention the change or schedule an appointment with a veterinarian.

There are two important points to consider here:

1. *Old age is not a disease.* If there is a problem, there is some specific cause for it, and you should discuss your pet's problem with your veterinarian.

2. *Even older pets have a right to a good quality of life*—just as human beings do. Those who love their pets have an obligation to identify what's really going on. In the case of swayback or similar symptoms, the changes in mobility may be—and often are—signals of a much more serious problem, such as a tumor!

True Stories from the Front Lines

Mandy, a 2-year-old Golden Retriever, had some scabs and matted neck hair. This only came to light as a result of her owner's purposeful petting. Mandy's owner noticed the change and immediately called my office; after examining Mandy, we were able to determine that the skin problems were a consequence of an emerging food allergy. Mandy was allergic to corn, a common ingredient in processed dog foods. We got her diet on track—and the allergic reaction disappeared. What would have happened if the owner had waited six months or a year to mention the symptoms of imbalance to us—or hadn't mentioned them at all?

Snooey was an 8-year-old, male Siamese cat that was overweight. His owner noticed that Snooey had started to slow down and was no longer playing around and jumping on his cat tree the way he used to, but did not call the veterinarian to discuss the problem. Time passed, and Snooey's owner noticed that Snooey was no longer coming around to be stroked and petted. At this point, she brought him to me for an examination—and we learned that Snooey had been suffering from arthritis in his lower back. Fortunately, I was able to get him on a better diet (to help him lose a little weight) and begin an acupuncture treatment that helped with the arthritis.

The Art of Balance

Remember, balance is the key to health, no less for animals than for people. Each of the changes listed on the preceding checklist might signal some kind of imbalance that deserves closer examination.

Signs of imbalance should be discussed with your veterinarian. *But you can only discuss the signals if you notice them in the first place!* That's why it's so important to make purposeful petting a part of your regular *daily* routine with your pet. You should know your pet better than anyone else. If you practice purposeful petting each and every day, you'll begin to develop a greater and greater sense of clarity about whether or not your pet is in balance. *Your pet is counting on you to notice this . . . and to schedule regular checkups with a qualified veterinarian who can help you by spotting things you may not notice due to your familiarity with your animal.*

Key Points to Remember

Make purposeful petting a part of your daily routine with your pet, and keep these key points in mind:

- Notice physical changes.
- Notice changes in energy.
- Notice changes in demeanor and behavior.
- Talk about these changes with your veterinarian!

Chapter 3

The Five Temperaments

What is your dog or cat really like? This is not an idle question about whether your pet is shy or outgoing, frisky or mellow, happy or grumpy. This question gets at your pet's essence—her core being. What is your pet's intrinsic nature?

As it happens, your pawed companion's intrinsic nature influences not just her disposition, but also her body rhythms, behavior, physical constitution, and susceptibility to certain health problems. That's because pets, just like people, contain principal forms of energy that influence how they feel and function on a daily basis, according to time-honored principles of Eastern medicine.

These principles maintain that there is a hidden but powerful life force—*chi*—within each living being and its surroundings. Ancient Chinese philosophers and physicians believed that five basic compositions occur in individuals; they identified these five compositions with five elements:

1. Fire
2. Earth
3. Metal
4. Water
5. Wood

Fire. Earth. Metal.

Water. Wood.

Because they noticed similarities between the characteristics of these natural elements and specific organ systems in the body, as well as similarities between the rhythms of the natural world and the inner workings of the body, they developed a concept of wellness that begins with these five elements. By learning and identifying how each pet is classified under this system, you may be able to learn where that pet is strongest or most vulnerable, and you may learn how to harness these deep, internal tendencies. An understanding of this ancient system can help you to get a clearer sense of the physical ailments your pet is prone to develop, and can even give you insights on her personality and pre-disposition: timid or bold, relaxed or tense, laid-back or watchful. These insights can give you all kinds of insights that can help you become a better partner in the care of the animal in your life . . . and also help you to improve your relationship with your pet.

I'll come back to the five elements frequently throughout this book. Think of the role of the elements in this way: *The forces that guide the cycles of change that take place in nature—particularly phases of expansion, contraction, decay, renewal, and transformation—also occur within the bodies and minds of living, breathing creatures like you and your pet.* This is one reason why external elements such as food, herbs, and even other living beings can have such a powerful effect on the functioning of the body. Over the centuries, this idea has been proven time and time again, and has become known as the *Five Element Theory*, which links each principal element from nature to an organ system in the body . . . and to a specific temperament (or constitution) in both people and pets.

An Integrated Way of Looking at Wellness

According to Traditional Chinese Medicine, the five elements and their associated body organs don't operate in isolation. Just as the head bone is connected to the neck bone and the neck bone is connected to the shoulder bones, each organ that's associated with a particular element is linked to another organ that's associated with a different element. This system is in accordance with literally centuries of research and observation in the Eastern world.

Let's say your "Earth" dog is suffering from persistent vomiting—a stomach problem. If the underlying condition is undiagnosed and untreated, the illness may end up affecting the small intestine, which is associated with the Fire element, or the large intestine, which is associated with the Metal element. Of course, all of these organs are part of the digestive system. Everything is interconnected! That may seem like an obvious point, but you'd be surprised how often this concept eludes Western veterinary science.

The previous example illustrates one of the critical differences between Eastern and Western veterinary medicine: While a Western vet might treat the "stomach" problem in isolation with medication designed to reduce nausea or eliminate harmful bacteria in the stomach, a vet who practices Eastern techniques might use herbs or acupuncture along key *meridians* (energy channels) in the body to fortify the stomach or to restore it to a more balanced state of *chi*.

Which Is the Dominant Element?

While all of the elements relate to each other and are present in all living beings, one element is usually dominant, shaping and defining that particular creature. Because the theory is that each element corresponds to a set of personality and behavioral traits in each person or pet, as well as to specific organ systems, this belief system has led to the establishment of certain temperament types based on the characteristics associated with each of the five elements in nature.

In other words, your pet's dominant element tells you a lot about what your pet is really like. I refer to your pet's dominant element as your pet's *temperament* or *type*.

Determining Your Pet's Dominant Element

Understanding your pet's type will shed light on the situations under which she may feel stress or tension. It will help explain why your pet friend responds better to specific remedies or prefers certain conditions and environments.

Moreover, identifying your pet's inherent makeup can give you advance notice of behavior and physical problems that are likely to develop in the future as she gets older.

Knowing your pet's true nature will also help you put the principles of *feng shui* into practice so you can moderate and balance the flow of *chi* in and around your pet.

To get a pulse on your pet's inherent type, take this quiz, which is based on the tenets of Traditional Chinese Medicine:

1. On a good day, how would you describe your pet's personality?

A) She is alert, happy, excitable, and energetic.

B) She is gentle, calm, stable, and friendly.

C) She is reserved, accepting, and disciplined.

D) She is curious, watchful, pensive, and self-contained.

E) She is powerful, aggressive, and bold.

2. How would you describe your pet's interactions with people?

A) She's typically happy and loving to everyone; she is a truly friendly animal.

B) She's gentle, calm, and sociable, and loves to play.

C) She's typically reserved, unsocial, aloof, and wise.

D) She is curious and picky about people, but comfortable with some; she often prefers to play alone.

E) She is aggressive, self-assured, and constantly on the move around others.

3. Which of the following best describes your pet's eating style?

A) She is an unfocused grazer who would generally prefer to play than eat.

B) She is a creature with a fierce and seemingly constant appetite; she overeats almost anything.

C) She prefers a set feeding schedule and consumes just enough for her body's needs.

D) She is a discretionary diner who waits for perfect conditions and doesn't eat a serving all at once.

E) She is a hearty eater who wants to eat first and whenever her owners eat; she often has food-driven aggression.

4. What does your pet friend most like to do with you?

A) She loves to romp and jump around in an unfocused manner.

B) She goes with the flow and loves to do anything to please you.

C) She is content to just hang out and observe what's going on.

D) She loves to walk and check out the scenery.

E) She likes to run and play rough, especially with rope toys or anything involving a tug of war.

5. When exposed to new people or places, your pet typically reacts with:

A) Indiscriminate excitement.

B) Mellowness.

C) Caution, often being slow to warm up.

D) Curiosity, getting her nose right into the action.

E) Boldness and aggression, often reacting quickly to stimulation.

6. **When the pet member of the family is sleeping, she usually seems:**

A) Erratic, alert to noises, and twitchy, as she appears to dream with movement.

B) Content and peaceful; she is truly a sound sleeper.

C) Easily aroused or awakened; she is a very light sleeper.

D) Relaxed but easily disturbed by events in the environment.

E) On guard or easily startled; she often awakens in fear.

7. **When you are upset with your pet, how does your pet typically respond?**

A) She tries to lick you and make things better.

B) She bows her head and becomes submissive.

C) She seeks solitude and retreats from you.

D) She is obedient, is eager to correct her misbehavior, and pays extra attention to you.

E) She is bold and stoic, taking your scolding in stride and showing little reaction.

8. **How does your dog or cat usually react to stressful or fear-provoking situations?**

A) She bolts, running away in fear.

B) She hides or crouches down, trying to make herself small.

C) She avoids conflict, staying on the outskirts of the situation.

D) She snoops or hangs around the scene, trying to see what's going to happen.

E) She reacts aggressively, often with an instinct to bite.

9. How is your pawed companion typically around other animals of the same species?

A) Playful and highly sociable.

B) Subdued, not wanting to really interact.

C) Very aloof, not wanting to acknowledge the other creatures' presence.

D) Curious, sniffing heavily; she wants to get involved.

E) Aggressive and competitive; she often jumps or lunges at other pets.

10. What is your pet's favorite place in your home?

A) Wherever the action is.

B) A cool, low place that's close to where you are.

C) Out of high-traffic areas; she likes to observe from a prime vantage point.

D) On the bed, close to you.

E) Close to doorways and other exits.

Now tally up how many times you selected A, B, C, D, or E as the answer that best characterizes your pet.

If you chose mostly **As,** your pet is a "Fire" type.

If you chose mostly **Bs,** your pet is an "Earth" type.

If you chose mostly **Cs,** your pet is a "Metal" type.

If you chose mostly **Ds,** your pet is a "Water" type.

If you chose mostly **Es,** your pet is a "Wood" type.

Invoking the Elements

Not surprisingly, each of the five elements has a set of personality, behavioral, and constitutional characteristics. Here's how they stack up next to each other.

Element	Personality Traits	Disposition	Favorite Activities	Associated Organs	Feng Shui Color
Fire	Lively, charismatic, vocal, aware, enthusiastic, devoted, alert	Attentive, active	Running, interacting with others, performing obedience exercises, being the focus of attention	Small intestine, heart	Red
Earth	Supportive, relaxed, stable, sociable, poised, attentive	Gentle and calm	Wants to do everything with her owner and activities are conducive to making her owner happy	Spleen/pancreas and stomach	Yellow
Metal	Discerning, disciplined, reserved, accepting	Likes definition, structure	Performing obedience exercises, engaging in structured activities	Lungs and large intestine	Silver/Gold
Water	Watchful, candid, curious, particular, self-contained, and self-sufficient	Resistant to and fearful of change; prefers to be left alone	Likes to do things on its own, marches to its own drum, doesn't like organized exercise	Kidneys and urinary bladder	Blue
Wood	Confident, assertive, bold, competitive, powerful	Very aggressive; loves action, movement, and adventure; likes to be first	Aggressive play with pull toys, using its mouth to play games	Liver and gallbladder	Green

Fire: Joy and Excitement

In the natural world, fire has the capacity to generate heat and light as well as ignite passion and excitement. Similarly, a "Fire" pet is filled with warmth, energy, joy, charisma, affection, expressiveness, enthusiasm, intuition, empathy, and excitement.

These pets' feelings are often readily apparent; they tend to wear their "hearts on their fur." They also are typically very alert. Dogs in this elemental category are extremely devoted and enjoy running, performing obedience exercises, or doing just about anything with their owners that involves interaction or being the focus of attention—that's how much they treasure intimacy. A similar dynamic comes into play with cats in this group.

Imbalances are most likely to occur in the heart, circulatory system, and small intestine, particularly as the pet gets older, or during times of pronounced physical or environmental stress. Dogs or cats of this type can easily become hyperactive, anxious, or agitated if they're left alone for too long or if they're overstimulated. A deficiency in these organs can make pets become confused, panicky, or selfish, or cause them to startle easily.

Earth: Involvement and Connection

Like the soil that covers the ground, earth has the ability to provide stability, nourishment, and sustenance as trees, flowers, and other plants take root and grow skyward. Similarly, an "Earth" personality tends to have practical, grounded intelligence; a desire to please and nurture; a keen sensitivity to people's moods; and great tracking skills. Earth types tend to be clannish, social creatures: They are loyal, obedient, gentle, relaxed, stable, sociable, poised, and attentive; they often want to do everything they can with their owners and anything they can to make their owners happy. In other words, they like to be involved and accommodating, and they value security and predictability very highly.

Dogs or cats of this type often have trouble with their spleen, pancreas, and stomach. If they develop an imbalance, these Earth types can become overprotective, meddlesome, worried, or overbearing. Or they may become clinging, scattered, or fawning or may experience dramatic fluctuations in appetite, weight, or physical activity levels.

Pingo, a Toy Poodle

Type: Fire

Personality traits: Always lively, aware, and happy to see her owner; constantly wanting to be the center of attention; very devoted to her family.

Social habits: Loves to play with anyone; gets along with most dogs she meets.

Physical energy level: Very high; always has plenty of energy and enthusiasm; can be hyperactive at times and has trouble settling down and disengaging from play mode. Even while sleeping she twitches and makes noises.

Favorite activities: Running, being the focus of attention, and playing with her owners.

Sam, a Labrador Retriever

Type: Earth

Personality traits: A loyal, calm, gentle giant who is always eager to please and goes with the flow at home.

Social habits: Likes to snuggle up to people or play a game of fetch with his owner; has blended well into a family with two cats and a small mixed-breed female dog. Loves to lie around all day in a cool spot off the master bedroom.

Physical energy level: Erratic; enjoys playing ball, but only if it is not too early in the morning.

Favorite activities: Lounging around the house in a cool spot, snuggling, and eating.

Metal: Structure and Discipline

Sharp, hard, and strong, metal provides structure and boundaries. Though it is often considered a man-made material, it is actually a pure substance that's derived from the earth. Like its counterpart in nature, a "Metal" type of pet is typically disciplined, reserved, discerning, orderly, calm, and composed, often bordering on aloof. More often than not, her energy is contained within.

Dogs or cats of this type like structure and routine; they have a great respect for authority, which is why they enjoy performing obedience exercises and structured activities such as a game of fetch. They like to have stability and one home; this is not a traveling pet.

Allergies, skin afflictions, and respiratory problems involving the lungs are common in these pets, as are symptoms related to the large intestine (such as constipation and diarrhea). An imbalance can cause a dog or cat of this type to become ritualistic, stoic, indifferent, or brooding. They may develop sloppy, elusive, persnickety, aimless, or resigned behaviors.

Water: Strength and Self-Sufficiency

Like underground hot springs, "Water" pets have reserves of strength that can be tapped if you delve far enough below the surface. These animals tend to be curious, perceptive, clever, watchful, sensible, self-possessed, enigmatic, and solitary by nature. They are generally resistant to and fearful of change. They are extremely loyal and committed to their owners. They tend to be skittish around new people, preferring to stay out of the limelight.

These creatures like to do things on their own. They move to the beat of their own drum. They don't enjoy organized activities or formal exercise; some pets of this type won't even let their owners brush them.

Kidney and bladder problems are common among these pets. When an imbalance occurs, a dog or cat of this type can become withdrawn, reticent, fearful, suspicious, or demanding. Other problems may be fussiness, fragility, phobic behavior, absent-mindedness, weakness, and fatigue.

Riley, a Rottweiler

Type: Metal

Personality traits: Mellow, a quick learner, keenly aware, intensely focused, sensitive to his owner, obedient, and content within himself. Not openly affectionate and does not seek a lot of petting.

Social habits: Can seem aloof; often acts disinterested and doesn't show or seek much affection; tends to ignore other dogs, as though he is above them.

Physical energy level: Low-key; happiest lying around the house, away from foot traffic.

Favorite activities: Hanging out in his favorite spot away from traffic and observing the action in the house; competing in agility contests.

Coco, a Domestic Shorthaired Cat

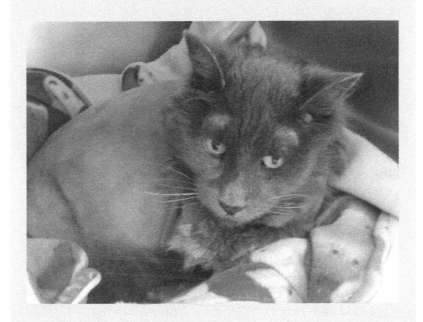

Type: Water

Personality traits: Curious, sometimes mischievous, unattached, independent, and watchful.

Social habits: Prefers to be left alone; runs and hides when strangers come over; won't even let her owner pet or brush her.

Physical energy level: Medium; can be slow to get moving after lying down for a while.

Favorite activities: Enjoys spying on the action in the house and playing with her toys for long periods.

Wood: Expansion and Resiliency

Wood is supple, adaptive, expansive, and upwardly mobile; think of a tree growing up from the ground. It literally thrives under pressure. Similarly, a dog or cat with a "Wood" constitution is typically confident, assertive, competitive, possessive, resourceful, and highly motivated. These creatures love action, movement, and adventure and tend to be bold, assertive, and decisive, often engaging in the relentless pursuit of a task, whether it's chewing a bone or batting around a ball of string. They also enjoy aggressive play with pull toys or using their mouths to play games.

Dogs of this type tend to have a threatening bark and often lunge aggressively at people and other pooches; they may be wary and alert, ready to react to the slightest provocation. Cats of this type can be quick to lash out or strike and don't like unfamiliar people encroaching on their environment. Liver and gallbladder ailments are common among Wood types.

An imbalance can cause a dog or cat of this type to become aggressive, antagonistic, impulsive, and tyrannical. Other problems may be irritability, moodiness, sensitivity to noise, peevishness, or highly erratic behavior.

Temperaments Can Mix and Match

Many of these elemental traits and characteristics apply across different species, including human beings. (I hope you're not lunging aggressively at people, though, if you're a Wood type!)

Neither people nor their pets are a hundred percent of one composition or another. The majority of a temperament may be one type (such as Fire), but there could be some aspects of another type (such as Earth) mixed in. You may have picked this up from the results of the quiz.

These blends are often what make your pawed companion—and you—unique as an individual, similar to the way a genetic map does in the Western view of medicine. The precise pattern of these elemental influences, along with their continuously shifting course, is part of what makes each creature distinctive. As a result, no two pets of the same type are exactly alike because the secondary elements exert varying degrees of influence.

Isaac, a Large, Domestic Longhaired Cat

Type: Wood

Personality traits: Aggressive, bold, adventurous, clever, intense, self-assured, often ill-tempered and grouchy.

Social habits: Exerts a powerful presence in the family; can be antisocial (often hisses at anyone who approaches him); frequently engages in catfights.

Physical energy level: Active; constantly on the move. Often goes out on nightly escapades instead of sleeping at home.

Favorite activities: Playing biting games, fighting with other cats, and asserting his powerful presence wherever he goes. His favorite spot is blocking the front door.

In some instances, however, it can be very difficult to discern whether a particular behavior or symptom is due to a characteristic that's associated with a particular type or an imbalance in the natural workings of the body—which is why the trickier assessments are best left to a practitioner of Eastern disciplines.

Noticing and Harmonizing the Cycles

These elements—and the types that are associated with them—are by no means static. Just as their qualities shift in nature, they can shift within the physical body, too, whether it's your body or your pet's. These five elements interact in a number of complex ways.

For one thing, each type needs to be balanced by aspects of all the other types, including:

- The warmth, brightness, and vibrancy of Fire
- The supportiveness, nurturing, and connectedness of Earth
- The structure, precision, and tenacity of Metal
- The self-sufficiency, depths, and fluidity of Water
- The boldness, expansiveness, and ability to perform well under pressure that is characteristic of Wood

The elements all bolster, add to, or detract from one another, helping to shape each other in the process.

At the core of the Five Element Theory is the recognition that living beings continuously undergo a process of change, involving cycles of excess and deficiency, decay, renewal, and regeneration.

The reality is, there are three different cycles involving the elements:

1. **The productive cycle,** in which one element fuels or boosts an adjacent element.
2. **The domination cycle,** in which one element keeps another in check.
3. **The reductive cycle,** in which a particular element reduces the strength or composition of another element to restore balance.

The productive cycle.

In the productive cycle:

- Fire produces earth.
- Earth is used to make metal.
- Metal melts into water.
- Water produces wood.
- Wood produces fire.

At first, this may seem confusing, but it makes logical sense if you consider what produces that element in nature—that wood sparks fire, for example. In the domination cycle, by contrast:

- Fire melts metal.
- Metal (from, say, an ax) cuts wood.
- Wood drains the earth.
- Earth (as in soil) soaks up water.
- Water puts out fire.

The domination cycle.

And in the reductive cycle:

- Fire reduces wood.
- Wood reduces water.
- Water reduces metal.
- Metal exhausts earth.
- Earth reduces fire.

All of these cycles are at work in living systems. They intertwine in a network of connected processes that follows a clear, logical, step-by-step sequence that can help you to understand your own (and your pet's) interconnection with the environment.

Most pet owners, I realize, are not interested in the intricacies of the various cycles that flow from the Five Element Theory. They simply want to help their pets. The best way to do that is to balance *chi*, that vital energy that flows through all living beings as well as the

The reductive cycle.

environment that surrounds us, so that it promotes optimal functioning of all body systems and general health and well-being. I will examine the task of restoring this kind of balance in the later chapters of this book.

Chapter 4

You and Your Pet Affect Each Other's Energy

You are more powerfully connected to your pet and more likely to affect his well-being than you may realize.

Initially, many of the pet owners I work with are surprised to learn that what happens in their own lives can have dramatic effects on their pets' health and well-being—and vice versa. For some reason, this kind of interconnection may exist "under the radar" for certain people, who may not always notice its effects. The interconnection is there nonetheless, and you should try to understand it more fully. Once you bond with your pet, that bond affects your mutual energy flow and your shared quality of life. You and the pet you love are, in a very real sense, residents of the same shared life experiences.

As you saw in a previous chapter, the life energy you share with your pet is present everywhere. It is worth repeating here that there is energy in the environment flowing from every living organism. People and pets can *transmit* energy to other living creatures. This is a fact that many do not recognize, or they manage to overlook, when they consider their relationships with their pets.

This energy transmittal has guided many of the healing arts—for instance acupuncture, acupressure, herbal remedies, *Reiki* (pronounced "ray-key"), and healing touch. These are just a few examples of effective therapies that take advantage of the fact that an adjustment of energy can enhance the body's ability to heal itself. All of these therapies, in fact, operate on the principle that you can guide your body to use energy and conduct energy to thrive and establish balance.

Your pet's personal energy is guided and conditioned through forces that you know about, but you cannot touch. This is one reason it is so important that you recognize and learn to sustain good energy within yourself: for the sake of the animal you love!

The energy of human owners is the biggest factor influencing the inner workings that affect the energy and well-being of pets. Other people and other animals also affect the flow of energy, but nowhere near the degree that owners do. Without good interaction with you that supports a healthy flow of energy, your pet cannot mature and become a quality member of the family.

The environment is always in motion, and always affecting the flow of *chi*. Events can change a pet's life and energy. Your cat hears two cats fighting outside, and this affects his *chi* flow—and yours. You pet your cat to calm her down . . . and you improve the shared flow of energy between you. In big ways and small ways, you need to constantly help your pet cultivate and coordinate *chi* within his environment.

Ronnie

Arthur, a travel agent, was going through a series of work challenges. He worked from home and was experiencing a lot of stress because the company he worked for was facing a major financial crisis. Lately he was

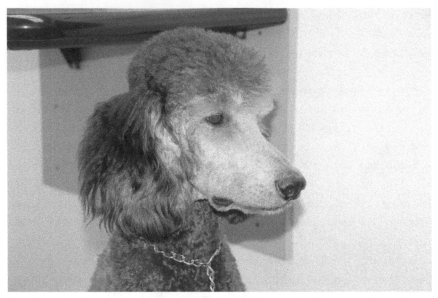

Ronnie needed a way to channel the stress that was causing his stomach problems.

spending more and more time in his home office—and enjoying that time less and less.

Interestingly, Arthur's Poodle, Ronnie, began losing weight around this time. Ronnie seemed weaker and less engaged than he had been in years past. During a discussion with me, Arthur wondered whether Ronnie was simply starting to show the effects of being a more mature dog. When he mentioned what was happening in his own world and talked about the challenges he was encountering at work, I asked for a chance to examine Ronnie in his home environment while Arthur was home. Arthur agreed, and we arranged a time for me to drop by for a visit.

I noticed immediately that Arthur's face was drawn and pale. He looked like he hadn't been getting much sleep. Arthur's office was located right next to Ronnie's feeding area, which was in turn very close to Ronnie's resting area during the day. I asked when he usually fed Ronnie, and Arthur admitted there was no set feeding schedule. "Sometimes I feed him at eight in the morning; sometimes I feed him at five," he explained. "It depends on what's happening during the day. I've had a lot to deal with lately."

It was at this point that I examined Ronnie. I found the poor dog suffering from stomach problems. Ronnie was "on and off" with his food.

He would sometimes look very interested in eating and then would turn away from his food after one bite.

Arthur was beside himself with worry. What could he do? His companion, his soul mate, was starting to waste away. I ran some diagnostic tests and found that Ronnie was developing ulcers within his stomach and intestines. What "caused" it? My suspicion was that stress played a role.

During a long discussion with Arthur, I shared my own interpretation of the situation: Arthur was going through a period of profound stress, and Ronnie, who loved Arthur deeply, was internalizing all the stress in the house. He was eating erratically and had no fixed feeding schedule, but that was only part of the problem. I believed that Ronnie's ulcerations of the stomach were stress induced.

Truth be told, Arthur was probably experiencing some stress-related problems of his own. I'm not an MD, of course, but even without attempting to make any kind of medical diagnosis, I had a feeling that Arthur had to find a way to calm down, get more sleep, get outside more, and restore a sense of order to his own life.

I asked Arthur whether he was willing, for his own sake and for Ronnie's, to make an effort to restore a routine with his dog—a routine that included a daily walk, regular feeding times with a change to a home-cooked diet that would be conducive to Ronnie's (Metal) composition (details will come later, in chapter 6, "Food: The Root of All Health"), and purposeful, focused indoor interaction with the dog at least once a day. I told Arthur that this was what Ronnie needed, which was absolutely true, and I told him that I thought he would benefit from these changes as well. That part was also absolutely true.

Arthur took my advice to heart and changed both his and Ronnie's daily behaviors along the lines that I suggested. A couple of months later, Arthur's stress-management techniques had improved dramatically. So had Ronnie's feeding schedule. There was a lot less stress in the house. The dog's ulcers had healed, and Arthur's habit of working fourteen- and sixteen-hour days had been curbed, if not eliminated entirely. There were still financial problems to confront at work, but I got the sense that Arthur was doing a better and more focused job of addressing those problems.

As you can see, the stress in Arthur's life at home was adversely affecting Ronnie's health. Initially, he didn't realize that his own work issues were a cause of health problems for the dog he loved. Once Arthur took responsibility for establishing a better balance in his own life, both dog and owner were a lot happier and a lot healthier. This story shows how making positive changes to the *chi* in the home environment can be a good choice for everyone.

A Powerful Connection to Your Pet

This much we know: A profound psychological and physical bond exists between humans and their pets, and this bond has an impact on life as we experience it. As I say, this bond, which is identified in Eastern terms as "mutual *chi*," is something pet owners may not always be able to put into words.

Here's one way to look at it. A person's energy runs through certain bodily pathways. These pathways can be compared to phone lines streaming through the body. Interestingly, this "phone system" is also available throughout the area *around* you—and the dial tone is always accessible. This "local" system is, in fact, a part of the much larger phone system that delivers service to the whole world—and the whole universe. Whenever a section of this phone system goes down, it finds other ways to manifest its power; it can not only bypass the area that caused a malfunction in the first place, but also instantly divert all the necessary functions to another pathway. By means of this "phone system" analogy, you can see that the mutual *chi* that flows between you and your pet is really part of *universal chi*. You can think of it as *mutual chi*, however, because it so powerfully supports the bond between pet and owner.

If you look to history, you see ample evidence for this powerful, enduring, and mutual connection between pet and owner; not only that, you also find that it has been a subject of discussion in literary works for centuries. Consider the following insights from animal lovers of years past—none of whom were proponents of Eastern medicine or philosophy:

This soldier, I realized, must have had friends at home and in his regiment; yet he lay there deserted by all except his dog. I had looked on, unmoved, at battles which decided the future of nations. Tearless, I had given orders which brought death to thousands. Yet here I was stirred, profoundly stirred, stirred to tears. And by what? By the grief of one dog.

—Napoleon Bonaparte, describing a battlefield scene:
a dog beside the body of his dead master,
licking the dead man's face and yelping

*I love cats because I enjoy my home; and little by little,
they become its visible soul.*

—Jean Cocteau

*If all the beasts were gone, men would die from a great loneliness of spirit,
for whatever happens to the beasts also happens to the man. All things are
connected. Whatever befalls the Earth befalls the sons of the Earth.*

—Chief Seattle of the Suquamish Tribe, in a
letter to President Franklin Pierce

*We need another and a wiser and perhaps a more mystical concept of
animals. . . . In a world older and more complete than ours they move
finished and complete, gifted with extensions of the senses we have lost or
never attained, living by voices we shall never hear. They are not brethren,
they are not underlings; they are other nations, caught with ourselves in the
net of life and time, fellow prisoners of the splendour and travails of the Earth.*

—Henry Beston

How do you and your pet affect each other's energy? For lack of a better term, I might be tempted to use the word *spiritual* to describe the deep, affecting emotional connection between some human beings and their pets. However you describe this effect, you know that the bond you establish with your pet, as the quotes above suggest, constitutes something remarkable, something special, and something quite different from the connection you have with, say, a television show, an automobile, or an Internet trivia game. The animal in your life is not a trinket; he is a companion of the soul.

You should not be surprised, then, that your own energy, your own health, and the quality of your own life are bound up with your pet's. And you should not shy away from acting on opportunities to improve energy, health, and quality of life whenever you encounter these opportunities.

No Quick Fixes

When I ask pet owners whether they want their pets to feel better and live longer, the answer I get is virtually always "Yes."

When I ask them whether they are willing to make long-term changes in their own daily routines, changes that will benefit both themselves and the animals that they're sharing their lives and their living quarters with, the responses are not always so clear.

In response, I may get questions in return, such as:

- "Exactly what kind of changes are you talking about?"
- "Why do I have to change my working hours for my dog or cat?"
- "Isn't there some treatment you can give my pet that will do the same thing as me changing my schedule?"

Of course, it's not surprising that some pet owners respond in this way. We live in a busy world, and finding ways to make changes in our own daily routine is not always easy. Yet there are times, as Arthur and Ronnie's case illustrates, when the only way to make meaningful long-term changes in the health and well-being of *both* pet and owner is to change what happens to both during the course of the average day. The reason for making that kind of mutual change is, I hope, obvious to you by now: *Owner and pet are connected in a special way.* Sometimes, to support your pet, you have to take action in a way that honors that connection.

If the owner is looking for a quick fix, something to do once and then walk away, then the results pet and owner experience are never going to be as positive as they could be. On the other hand, if the owner is willing to find ways to make modest, sustainable changes that will benefit both pet and owner, then substantial improvements in the overall quality of life of both pet and owner really are possible.

Ways to Support Mutual *Chi*

Following, you'll find a list of simple things that you can do for yourself and your pet that doesn't require you to turn your life upside down and at the same time supports mutual *chi*. You may already be doing some of these activities; others may be new to you. These changes are designed to be easy for you to incorporate into your schedule. All of them will help to improve your own energy flow—and the energy flow of your pet.

1. Establish a daily routine.

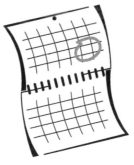

Establishing a daily routine will benefit both you and your pet—and it should be a high priority. A good routine is what makes everything else on this list possible. Spontaneity and unpredictability are fine, but you do need some kind of pattern in your daily life, and so does your pet. If your pet can't predict when feedings are going to happen, when walks are likely to take place, or when it's time to go to sleep, then both of you will have trouble generating a rhythm during the day.

No matter how erratic your schedule is, no matter how crazy your workday is, you can find some little ritual to build into your day—a ritual that your pet can predict and participate in, too. For instance, you can make an early-morning walk part of your daily routine. What sounds, motions, and actions typically precede that walk? Notice them and repeat them. Make them part of the fun of going for a walk so your pet knows that he has just entered the daily "space" of "getting ready to go for a walk."

Daily rituals make you and your pet feel confident and optimistic about the day. *Don't cheat yourself or your pet out of them!*

2. Establish regular feeding times and quantities.

This is, of course, one of the important daily rituals you'll want to establish with your pet. Many pet owners decide to synchronize their pets' eating times with those of the human family. (See chapter 6, "Food: The Root of All Health," for ideas on improving your pet's diet and establishing proper serving sizes.)

3. Develop a shared exercise routine.

If you take your dog for a walk twice a day, both of you will benefit. For cats, the exercise routine could involve play with a feather or fishing pole. Again, the key concept here is consistency. Establish something physical that you do with your pet every day—not something you do when you get around to it or something you do every other day. You don't have to get a massive workout: You're looking for a shared daily pattern of physical activity that's enjoyable to both of you.

4. Give your pet focused attention and positive interaction.

When you and your pet pay attention to each other, you create a win-win situation. At least once a day, for perhaps ten or fifteen minutes, you should try to spend some kind of quality, one-on-one emotional time with your pet. Speak positively, approvingly, and soothingly to your pet. Don't overwhelm your pet with attention, though, and don't let the attention become overbearing. Keep your interactions in balance over time; establish a good emotional connection.

5. **Reduce or omit the amount of time you spend watching television.**

Building your interaction time around sedentary moments spent watching television is not necessarily a good thing for either you or your pet. Some pet owners tell me their pets "love watching television." They may not realize that they're opening themselves up to potential problems with the circulation of *chi* in the home. (See chapter 5, "Identifying and Eliminating Negative Energy (*Sha*) from Your Home," for a fuller discussion of the circulation of *chi* in regard to watching television.)

6. **Practice stress and anger management if you need it.**

If your pet has to be in the same environment where you swear, shout, have temper tantrums, or encounter abuse, rest assured that this environment will have a negative effect on both you and him. Do what Arthur did: Find some way to change the behavior that negatively affects both you and your animal companion.

7. Be sure that your pet gets regular medical care.

Your pet needs medical care just as much as you do. The challenge is that your pet is not always very good at telling you what's wrong. This is why it's imperative that you not only observe your pet, but also provide him with regular medical attention. When a human being encounters a physical problem of some kind, he or she generally assumes that the doctor can fix it. You need to make the same assumption when the animal in your life encounters physical problems—and make an extra effort to find out what the potential problems are.

8. If you have only one pet and you spend a lot of time away from home, consider getting a second pet to keep the first pet company.

A second pet will help to establish harmony in the home, make everyone happier, and make *chi* stagnation in your home less likely.

The bond between humans and the animals they love and care for has been a part of our shared development for centuries. Whether you realize it at any given moment or not, you affect your pet, and he affects you, on the level of energy. In fact, there is an energy balance between you and all living beings you encounter. Sometimes the energy relationship may be hard to see, but it is there. Where such an energy bond exists, a channel for *chi* exists. In the larger sense, when you support the energy bond between yourself and your pet, you affect everything around you. By the same token, every living thing in your environment affects you. A plant in your living room that doesn't look lush can pull away *chi* from you, your pet, and anyone who enters the room.

Of course, figuring out the cause of a blockage of *chi* is not always easy. I prefer to start by looking at your relationship with your pet first . . . and then I will look at ways to improve *chi* flow in the home environment. Let's face it: Improving your relationship with your pet is a lot more fun than redecorating your home.

> *Life begets life. Energy begets energy. It is by spending oneself*
> *that one becomes truly rich.*
>
> —Sarah Bernhardt

Chapter 5

Identifying and Eliminating Negative Energy (*Sha*) from Your Home

Your living environment not only has the potential to help you tap a limitless well of psychic and physical energy on behalf of you and your pet—it also has the potential to block, attack, or even destroy this life-giving flow of power.

Unfortunately, many people live within environments where natural or man-made settings obstruct, deplete, degrade, or destroy *chi*—and they don't even know what is happening. These spaces are subject to a dynamic that sucks away the life force. That negative dynamic, which is just as real and just as important to understand as the dynamic that energizes and restores us, is called *sha* (pronounced "shaw"). *Sha* is an invisible circumstance that may be detrimental to both you and your pet. These circumstances can change the flow of energy and can really be a detriment to your pet's ability to adapt to the environment. With *sha*, it may even seem like subliminal messages are flowing through your pet's body. Some people might say that they are just experiencing bad luck, but some circumstances go deeper than bad luck. Circumstances that produce *sha* can be found in your natural surroundings and are not man-made—for instance, electrical lines that course over your property. To the innocent eye, power lines might not seem like any problem. But to the Eastern practitioner, this is a definite no-no. As your pet runs

An arrow is typically used to describe *sha*. As this energy pierces internal and external living environments, it creates imbalance and disharmony.

across your yard, she may come into contact with the potentially bad energy radiating from these power lines. The electrical lines are definitely modifying and changing the positive energy that otherwise moves freely in the yard. In many cases, a pet cannot handle these abrupt changes in the environmental flow of energy.

In the case of the power lines, I might ask you to have your pet play in another portion of the property instead of being near these wires. Small changes like this can create major benefits in a pet's life.

Mattie's Problems with *Sha*

Mattie, a 7-year-old tabby cat, loved to sleep on the TV set in her owner Brian's new apartment. He left the TV on all day so she could enjoy the warmth that emanated from the set and also the company of the television program that was on. During Mattie's younger years, Brian had initially left the TV on because she was enamored by the television and seemed to sit and watch along with Brian.

Brian had recently moved into this apartment, and Mattie, his best friend for the past seven years, had moved with him. After only three weeks in the new living environment, however, Brian could not escape the sensation that something was very different about Mattie's behavior.

Normally alert, playful, and a bit of a scamp, Mattie was now lethargic, withdrawn, and less likely to interact with Brian when he came home from work. "She just lounges on top of the TV all the time," Brian said when he called me, "and she doesn't even seem to know I'm there. I know there's nothing wrong with relaxing, but she just doesn't seem like the same cat I had before we moved. I used to watch television when I got home in the old apartment, too, and she'd come and play with me while I did. But now when I sit down at the end of a long day at work, Mattie just stays perched on top of the set."

In Brian's previous apartment, his boxy, midsized TV had been set into the top shelf of a series of bookshelves, and had been inaccessible to Mattie. Mattie had often slept in front of a heating vent, and Brian knew that she loved this spot because it was warm. In the new environment, there was no heating vent for Mattie to sleep next to. So, the TV became its replacement.

When I heard this much, I thought I just might have all the information I needed. Unfortunately, I didn't, and it was at this point that I missed an opportunity to improve Mattie's situation.

Instead of asking to visit Brian's apartment in person, which is what I should have done, I gave him a couple of suggestions over the phone. I asked him to turn off the TV during the day; to spend less time watching it in the afternoon and evening; to move the TV to a spot where Mattie could not easily climb on top of it; and to set up a cat tree in a window that received a lot of sunshine during the day.

A week later I got a call from Brian. He had done everything I'd suggested, and Mattie was now spending a great deal of time during the day sunning herself on the new cat tree. Brian himself was watching less TV. And there was now no way for the cat to lounge on top of his set when it was on. All of that was fine; however Mattie was just as lethargic and antisocial as she'd been before Brian had made these changes.

At this stage, a veterinarian who had been trained in the Western medical tradition might have asked Brian to bring Mattie in for an examination. If that had happened, the veterinarian would have uncovered no meaningful physical symptoms and probably would have told Brian there was nothing to worry about—or informed Brian that the issues he was describing were simply Mattie's response to the aging process and could not be changed.

I felt I had to take a different approach. I knew that the problems Brian was describing didn't seem to be life-threatening, but I also knew that they appeared to have something to do with the recent change in Mattie's environment. Instead of asking him to bring Mattie in for a checkup in my office, I asked him to let me pay a visit to the living environment he shared with her.

Of course, I examined Mattie closely when I met her for the first time. She had no meaningful physical symptoms that I could make out. I asked Brian if I could take a look around the apartment. When I saw where Brian had set up the cat tree—in a hallway window that faced an oncoming road—I realized what I had to do. Brian and I moved the cat tree to another window that received ample sun during the day. We also reorganized his living room by moving his couch so that it was no longer a partial obstruction near the entryway, and we took some of the furniture out of the room.

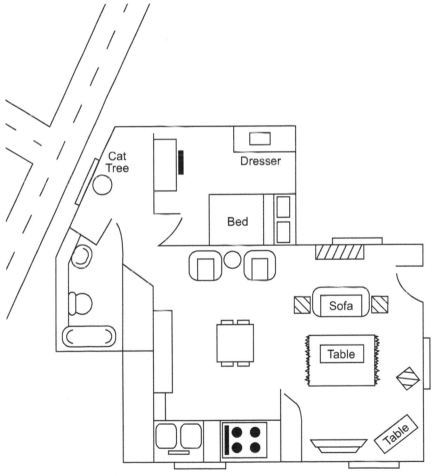

This drawing shows the layout of Brian's living room before he met with me.

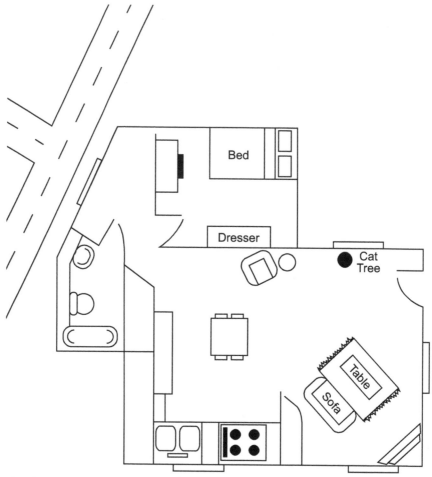

This drawing shows the layout of Brian's living room after we reorganized it to create an environment that eliminated negative *sha* by providing good *chi*.

Within a few weeks, Mattie had gotten back all the energy and friskiness she had had during her earlier time with Brian in the old apartment. She began greeting him and rubbing up against his leg when he returned from work each day. She was alert, aware, engaged, and happy. Her need for endless lounging appeared to have vanished as quickly as it had appeared.

Here are some questions to consider:

1. Why was it so important for me to examine not only Mattie, but also the apartment where she and Brian now lived?

2. Why did the initial placement of the cat tree fail to restore Mattie's energy and her eagerness to engage with Brian?

3. How had the television affected the flow of *chi* in Brian and Mattie's living environment?

4. Why, by contrast, did rearranging the furniture in the living room seem to help Mattie regain her energy?

These kinds of questions are typically overlooked or ignored by traditional Western veterinary science. This is a shame because the answers to questions like these reflect critical issues that can affect your pet's health and well-being—because *sha* can affect your pet's health and well-being. Let's look at each of these questions in turn.

1. **It was important for me to examine not only Mattie, but also her living environment, because *sha* manifests itself in physical spaces.**

   For instance, the direct approach of a road or a path can make it possible for *sha* to throw the *chi* in a living space out of balance. This was the case with Mattie's first cat tree. It was placed near a window that overlooked a road whose placement suggested a potential problem with *sha*. Of course, learning to recognize this kind of problem takes training and experience, and I'm not expecting you to be able to spot and resolve every problem with *sha* that presents itself in your world. What I want you to understand, though, is that some physical settings within your home are really likely to be trouble spots when it comes to *sha*. For instance, the first window where Brian set up Mattie's cat tree not only overlooked a road that directly approached the house, but also happened to be located in a T-shaped hallway intersection within the building. That's two potential *sha* problems in one place! T-shaped corridor intersections are a common entry point for *sha*, and should not be used as feeding or sleeping areas for your pet. In this case, the placement of the cat tree in this spot was keeping Mattie from rebounding and resuming her normal energy level.

2. **Brian's initial placement of the cat tree failed to help Mattie because he did not get an in-person assessment of the space by someone who knew how to identify potential problems with *sha*.**

I heard what Brian said was happening and felt that I could quickly remedy the situation without going into more depth. However, if I had taken the opportunity to visit the apartment before making any suggestions, I likely would have sped up Mattie's recovery. I would have quickly noticed the problems with the window area in question and located a different warm spot where Mattie could play and spend her time.

3. **The television affected the flow of *chi* in Brian and Mattie's living area in several important ways.**

  • First, the TV was in a room that was crowded with too much furniture. There was a couch, a small futon, two chairs, an entertainment center with a stereo, a coffee table, an end table, and a cat tree. And there were other odds and ends, such as an exercise stepper. Brian felt that this apartment was just a transitional place for them and before long he would move into a larger place he could call his own. He had a hodgepodge of furniture that he had collected over the years. Though Brian may seem frugal, there was just too much going on in the apartment and he even told me that it seemed a little cramped. Cramped, crowded, and overstuffed surroundings can and do attract *sha*.

  • Second, the TV itself was an angled, edged, sharp surface with different forces of energy emanating from it. These kinds of surfaces can act as magnets for *sha*.

  • Third, the television was on too much of the time! Constant, numbing exposure to television not only has a negative effect on your outlook on life, but it can also have a negative effect on the *chi* levels that you and your pet experience. By the way, the same goes for microwave ovens and many other electric appliances; they often lead to depletions of *chi*.

4. **Rearranging the furniture in the living room helped Mattie and Brian regain their energy for one simple reason: Good decisions about physical space can minimize or eliminate the influence of *sha*.**

By reorganizing the room, we reduced the total number of furniture elements, thereby decreasing the sense of crowding that can attract *sha*. We also compensated for the angled, hard-edged elements of the room with drapes, plants, and wall hangings. The end result was a more peaceful, more serene, and less chaotic space. This newly configured floor plan left both pet and owner feeling more alive and engaged.

Although it may seem easy to seek and rectify *sha* problems, there are times when the challenges of *sha* can really be difficult to see and identify! Not all cases are similar to or as easy to fix as Brian and Mattie's situation, but this is a good example of how clutter can get out of control and can truly cause a negative influence on your pet. Remember, your pet has little or no control over her environment; you are the guardian and you have to establish the right living conditions for your pet.

Initial Skepticism about the Existence of *Sha*

Some pet owners who come to me for help are initially skeptical of or resistant to the idea that there is even such a thing as *sha*, and feel as though discussing *sha* means endorsing some strange or dangerous realm of paranormal activity. I have devoted some of the later material in this chapter to addressing the concerns of pet owners who feel this way. If this is how you feel about *sha*—if talk of a negative energy dynamic in your living space sounds like superstition, trickery, or any other unhealthy process—I hope you'll read the upcoming discussion about *sha* with an open mind. I will give you the following helpful insights:

1. Explain what *sha* is.
2. Determine how you can recognize *sha* as a reality in your world.
3. Examine how the effects of *sha* on the living space that you and your pet share are so potentially serious.

If you look into the history of Eastern philosophies, you will see that *sha* has been a topic of serious discussion for thousands of years. If it were all a delusion, we would have neither the track record, nor the present-tense experience with *sha*, that we do.

Initial Confusion about How to Correct *Sha*

Other pet owners are less skeptical about *sha,* but are more likely to be confused about what to do next. They accept the principle that *sha* can have damaging effects on their own health and on the health of their pets and have a simple question for me: *What can someone who is not well versed in the principles of* feng shui *do to counteract* sha? Every pet owner wants to do his or her best to help out a family member. There are real threats in the environment and you want to take care of these things, just as you would protect and nurture a baby. What, at a minimum, should you do?

If you fall into this category, rest assured that I'll do my best to answer this important question for you at the conclusion of this chapter.

Sha Is Real!

Chi is found everywhere in a home. Chi can even be found radiating from a home's inhabitants in the form of personal Chi. Your personal Chi and your home's Chi complement each other. . . . A hostile or unorganized living space creates chaos. This chaotic Chi will impact your personal attitude each time you find yourself inside of the chaotic room. As a result, your home may be the cause of much unnecessary stress in your life.

—From *Happy Home Zone Web site,* "Feng Shui and Home Design," *www.fengshui.happyhomezone.com*

Some people initially make the mistake of thinking of *sha* as some otherworldly, demonic energy, but that's really not what I'm talking about. It is a *vacuum* of positive *chi*—a vacuum that's intense enough to push people and animals out of balance and cause problems.

Sha is simply chi that is not organized in a way that's conducive to good health. It is *chi* that attacks and undermines your body, and it does not support or sustain you. If you doubt the existence of this kind of *chi,* then you doubt that energy can have both constructive consequences and destructive consequences.

Think of *chi* with constructive consequences as "good" energy. This kind of *chi* circulates gently through a living space, or any space, in curves and waves. When a living space is arranged in such a way that it forces *chi* into sharp angles and straight lines, however, that "good" energy no longer circulates gently. Instead, it accumulates in points and barbs. Those points and barbs act like arrows, and they can have unsettling or even dangerous impacts on you and your pet. These are "secret arrows" that you cannot see and thus cannot avoid—until you suffer their ill effects.

These "secret arrows" are everywhere, and, unfortunately, pet owners usually don't notice them. In the account of Brian and Mattie, I mentioned that one of the problems with the first location where Brian set up the cat tree was that it was located within a T-shaped intersection in the home. Another problem was that it faced an oncoming road that took the form of a straight line. I'm reminding you of this part of the story because streets, roads, highways, and driveways that proceed toward you in a straight line really are potentially serious sources of *sha*. If you doubt this, think for a moment about which home you would rather own: One that is located on a winding, secluded country road, or one that is positioned as the "target" of a straight, busy street? For most people, the secluded home positioned on the gently winding road feels "right" in a way that a home located at the terminus of a dead end does not.

Some of the most skeptical pet owners I've met have quickly become believers when we worked together to make changes in their physical environment and solved their *sha* problems. The "secret arrows" in a living space are real. The trick is to notice them and find ways to counteract them!

Ways to Recognize *Sha* in Your Environment

Here's the good news: You probably don't have to remodel your home, or move, in order to reduce problems with *sha*. All you really have to do is become more sensitive to the most common situations that *produce sha* . . . and then be willing take some common-sense steps to address those situations.

Sometimes pet owners ask me for a single piece of advice that they can use to make a living space "*sha*-proof." In fact, there's no way to make any space completely "*sha*-proof"—hurricanes and tornadoes, for instance, may intrude at moments you least expect. Even so, you can follow one principle as you try to promote the gentle, healing flow of *chi* in the living space you share with your pet. Here it is:

The more complex and angular the surface of your living space is, the more likely it is that you're going to have a problem with sha.

Chi likes smooth, flowing surfaces. Its healthy flow is diminished when it is forced into corners or around sharp edges. With this in mind, you should always look for ways to minimize the effects of edges and angles, and you should also be on constant lookout for ways to emphasize rounded, smooth surfaces. Strategically placed drapes, curtains, and screens can help you minimize *sha* problems with the corners in a room. Similarly, placing furniture in the middle of the room can definitely cut off the even flow of *chi*. This is basically placing angles in the center of the space!

This is the single, guiding principle that is most likely to help you as you evaluate your pet's—and your own—susceptibility to *sha*. Even if you don't yet feel you're an expert on *feng shui*, this one idea of emphasizing smooth, rounded surfaces and deemphasizing angular ones will help you to support an environment of harmony and balance.

The following sections cover other issues for you to consider when addressing problems with *sha*.

Look at Sleeping, Eating, and Resting Areas First

Sleeping, eating, and resting areas are a good place to start when evaluating the *chi* your home. As you have seen, if the place where your pet sleeps, eats, or rests is the "target" of a straight hallway—if it faces a window directly over a straight, oncoming street or driveway, or if it is located at the center of a T-intersection within the home—you should make it a priority to find a better space for your pet to sleep, eat, or rest.

By the same token, sleeping, eating, or resting areas that are located near garbage receptacles or in a bathroom should be moved. A pet owner I once worked with told me that his dog was lethargic and suffered from low energy; when I examined the home, I saw that the dog's eating area was located in the bathroom! This was an open invitation for problems with *sha* because waste eats up *chi*. When we moved the dog's food and water dishes to another part of the house and made some changes in the dog's diet, the lethargy disappeared. Take this important principle into account when deciding where your pet will eat and sleep.

Turn off the TV

As I mentioned earlier, minimizing exposure to television is a good "*sha* safety" step for both pet and owner. My personal experience is that pet owners who routinely spend extensive periods in front of the television set leave themselves and their pets open to potentially serious problems with *sha*. I realize that television is popular and that many worthwhile programs appear on TV, and I'm certainly not suggesting that you discontinue television viewing permanently. All I'm saying is that you should look for reasons to turn *off* the television rather than look for reasons to turn it *on* when you walk into a room.

Be Sensitive to Traffic and Noise

The traffic patterns in a home and the amount of noise generated in a given space can also produce *sha*. If a space is too busy, too hectic, or too noisy, you should think twice before you make that space a centerpiece of your pet's daily routine—or your own. Rooms that feature high noise from streets or highways are a common source of problems with *sha*.

One pet owner asked me to have a look at his Labrador Retriever who was becoming seriously overweight. After a brief examination of the dog's living space, I saw that his sleeping pillow was set up in a hallway, right in the middle of the family's major avenue for foot traffic! When we changed the dog's sleeping area to a calmer, more peaceful place in the house, his low-energy problem disappeared—and before too long, so did his weight problem.

Look at the Flow of *Chi*

To promote a healthy flow of *chi* in your living environment, the entry and exit points in a given room should be left open and unobstructed:

- Place couches and chairs to the sides of entryways.
- A bed should not face a door.
- Minimize or eliminate elements that block the natural flow of energy.

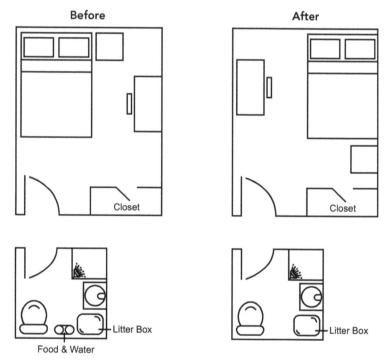

By taking the food out of the bathroom and not having the bed face the bathroom, we were able to restore harmony and balance to this environment.

Listen to What Multiple Pets Are Telling You

If you have more than one pet and you notice that they routinely have conflicts that are located predictably in a single location within the home, there's a very good chance that you've got a "secret arrow" in this spot that was produced either by the physical configuration of the space or by the interactions between the pets themselves.

Sha problems that produce conflicts between pets may well be related to the pets' shared environment that you've chosen as the feeding area. Consider establishing a separate feeding area for each pet.

Little Changes Can Make a Big Difference!

Even modest changes in the environment that you share with your pet can have a big impact when it comes to minimizing or eliminating *sha*. Start simple, and if you suspect that you have a problem in the environment that modest changes haven't fixed, get help and advice from a professional who's qualified to help you improve the flow of "good" *chi* in your home.

Chapter 6

Food: The Root of All Health

The old adage that "you are what you eat" applies just as much to your pet as it does to you. You may be feeding your pet what is advertised as being best for his body, but there is a good chance your pet would benefit from foods that are uniquely suited to his temperament. As you shall see in this chapter, some of the highly processed pet diets advertised today have serious limitations when it comes to supporting pet health. This is evidenced by the epidemic of obesity that has befallen pets in the United States and other countries.

The more pure, unprocessed nutrients you can put into your dog's or cat's diet, the better your pet will be able to use these nutrients to fulfill its body's essential functions, instead of just storing them as body fat or passing them as waste products. Your pet will do even better if you can customize its diet based on its temperament and circumstances. I'll give you some advice on how to do that in this chapter, too.

We should start by understanding that food is the vital *chi*, the root of all health. Unfortunately, many bargain-hungry pet owners act as though diet is largely irrelevant to an animal's well-being. Ask some pet owners to define a healthy dietary change for their pet, and you may get a response like, "Buy a different brand of dry food" or "Switch from dry food to wet food," or even "Cut down on the ice cream!"

The dietary choices for people's pets are often determined by their own habits and their sense of what is and isn't convenient. What is habitual and convenient for pet owners, however, does not always match up with the resources their pets need for a long and healthy life. I believe that food is among the most important of those resources—and that's why long-term changes in nutrition are such a big part of my approach to animal wellness.

Of course, long-term dietary changes usually require the consent, cooperation, and involvement over time of a pet's owner. That's sometimes a challenge because many of those owners are initially a little skeptical about the changes that I propose. They're not convenient, they aren't familiar, and they sometimes cost more than what the owner is usually doing to feed his or her pet. It usually takes a while for people to realize that there really is a benefit to going outside of their comfort zone when it comes to feeding their pets. But there definitely is such a benefit!

All of the dietary changes I suggest in order to promote pet health are based on proven healing principles —not on advertising campaigns, passing trends, or urban legends. I make a point of insisting on good dietary habits for the pets I care for, for one simple reason: The food your pet eats has a profound effect on his health and well-being, just as what you eat has a major impact on your own health.

To eat is a necessity, but to eat intelligently is an art.

—*La Rochefoucauld*

What Is the Difference between Whole and Processed Foods?

Whole foods are the raw materials that you see in the grocery store or on farms. They are the meats, vegetables, and grains that are still in their whole, fresh form and are waiting to be prepared into a meal for a living organism. *Processed foods*, on the other hand, are exactly what the name suggests: heavily processed products. Any claims that these products offer optimal nutritional value when compared to whole foods should be regarded with healthy skepticism.

Whole foods provide the raw materials that your pet's body needs. On the other hand, processed foods use the ingredients that are mathematically adequate for the pet but may not be the most optimal for his or her health. Pet food manufacturers are using available raw materials and balancing them accordingly—in a way that makes sense to them from a competitive and economic standpoint. You must always remember that the pet food companies are in competition with each other to sell food that is adequate *and* competitive for the market. With this in mind, they are taking the lowest-cost raw materials, such as meat and poultry by-products, and putting them into your pet's foods. When using less-than-optimal sources of raw materials for the foods, are you putting your pet at risk for potential exposure to toxins? These toxins may include pesticides, spoiled raw materials, drug residues from meats, and a whole host of other questionable ingredients.

When processed food is produced, it is cooked under high temperatures for long periods of time, then made into kibbles and baked or put into a can, and then shipped for hundreds or even thousands of miles. This long-term process can easily destroy the nutrients that your pet's body needs, and make the digestibility of his food less than optimal.

With whole foods, you are giving your pet fresh foodstuffs that have not been broken, sealed, or shipped across the country. The advantage is obvious—and if you doubt that much, all you have to do is ask yourself how healthy you would be if you avoided *all* freshly prepared fruits, vegetables, meats, and grains in favor of a diet that consisted of, say, beef jerky, potato chips, Tang, and a daily multivitamin tablet. Technically, you might be meeting all your requirements for vitamins and minerals, but in reality there would be something gravely wrong with the way you were eating if you were forced to keep to that diet for months or years on end.

Very often, an owner will change his or her pet's processed food and notice that the pet has quickly developed problems with diarrhea. Veterinarians treat this problem by suggesting a diet of chicken and rice. It works because the new food is whole, not processed. The pet would be a great deal better off if he simply continued to eat the chicken and rice!

When I share this perspective with pet owners, they're sometimes shocked. How could pet food companies sell them food that is not the best-possible diet for their animal? The answer—which many pet owners don't really want to hear—is that the pet food companies are only responding to what they, the pet owners, are saying that they want: convenience and low prices.

He that takes medicine and neglects diet, wastes the skill of the physician.

—*Chinese proverb*

Would You Eat the Way You Ask Your Pet to Eat?

It's a rare pet owner indeed who is willing to eat exactly what his or her pet is fed for even a single day. I've never met one who would agree to stick to the same human meal—say, spaghetti and meatballs with a glass of water on the side—for a month straight, with no variation.

How often do you ask your pet to endure the same stale meal choice, day after day, week after week, month after month, and year after year? How often do you give your pet meals that you would never eat? How likely are you to offer your pet a diet that is unremittingly boring, over-processed, and (perhaps worst of all) unlikely to promote healthy *chi* flow? These are not always popular questions, but I believe they are worth asking all the same. Another good question is this one: "Would you really consider changing from one brand of dry food to another brand of dry food to be a major positive dietary change?"

I'm afraid my own answer to that last question is no. What's more, I wouldn't be all that excited about getting fed from a can every day—and I don't think you would, either.

As a bet once I ate some dog biscuits in front of my cousin. I can't remember the name of them, but it's a popular brand, they come in four shapes (circle, triangle, square, and oval) and are pastel-colored. They are bloody horrible! . . . I pity dogs after that day.

—*Posting on the Snopes.com Internet message board*

When I ask pet owners why they feed their pets the same dreary meals day in and day out—things that they themselves would never consume—I sometimes get a quizzical look, as though the answer were obvious. When I do get an answer, it generally sounds like this: "Animals can't tell the difference—they don't know any better."

It's really astonishing to me how people can feel so close to their pets emotionally—and can at the same time be so distant from them on an issue that is so obviously connected to the pet's quality of life. Having worked with literally thousands of pets (and pet owners) over the years, I can assure you that pets are able to tell the difference between cheap, overprocessed food and food that is fresh, healthy, and varied. They do notice a change for the better in their diet—just as we would—and they do express gratitude to their owners for noticing that their diets need improving. (Many pet owners tell me that their pets "love" canned food, but my personal opinion is that they would love whole food even more if they were given a chance to eat it on occasion, and would also appreciate the break in the monotony of their processed diet.)

The big reason I choose to feed pets whole foods over processed foods is that the processed food has lost a lot of its nutritional *chi* due to overprocessing. The *chi* present in whole foods is quite dramatic, and promoting *chi* flow is what I focus on in this book. You are trying to harbor *chi* in order to increase your pet's health and vitality, and diet is an essential tool for doing that. Frankly, I find the idea of trying to improve a pet's health through exercise and interaction, while at the same time ignoring the fact that you're feeding the pet nothing but processed food, to be perplexing. Yet this is what most of the pet owners I talk to are inclined to do.

Getting pet owners to change their outlook about this issue is one of the main reasons I wrote this book. Improving the quality of your pet's food is one area where you really can help your pet tremendously. There are certain factors that affect pet health—such as genetics and pollution—that you cannot do anything about, but you can take advantage of ideas that help you to preserve and direct the invaluable energy source that is so often degraded in "pet food."

In this chapter, you'll get some background on the kinds of dietary changes I suggest for the animals I care for, as well some good advice on creating a healthy, varied diet for your pet.

Food and the Five Elements

I've already shared with you the five elements that influence your pet's temperament, or personality. Once again, they are:

- Metal
- Earth
- Wood
- Water
- Fire

As you know, it's very likely that one of these elements represents your pet's basic constitution and thus dominates your pet's behavior and demeanor. What you may not realize is that the foods you choose to feed your pet can have an important balancing effect on your pet's temperament, and can help improve your pet's well-being and longevity by improving his ability to harness and channel life-giving *chi*.

The productive cycle.

To understand this concept, it helps to understand some of the principles behind the five elements.

Productive cycles between the five elements include interactions where one element brings forth, supports, or sustains another element. For instance, you can think of Water sustaining Wood—because plants need water to grow. Similarly, Wood sustains Fire when it burns, Fire creates ash (that is, earth), and Earth brings forth Metal (because metal is mined). The idea that Metal sustains Water may seem a little far-fetched—until you think of a metal cup on a hot summer day: Pour a cold liquid into the cup and water will also form on the outside of the cup through condensation.

Domination cycles, despite the name, are not really about elements dominating one another, but rather about one element that can neutralize another by destabilizing it. Thus:

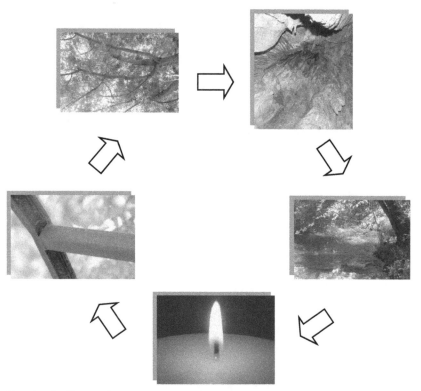

The domination cycle.

- Wood disrupts Earth (by rising through it).
- Earth obstructs Water (by stopping its flow).
- Water extinguishes Fire.
- Fire melts Metal.
- Metal (in the form of an axe) chops through Wood.

Reductive cycles counterbalance the destabilizing effects seen in the domination cycles—and are thus the cycles we're most interested in initiating by means of dietary change (and many other therapies). The whole point of altering an animal's diet is to reestablish balance!

The reductive cycles play out as follows:

- Water corrodes Metal.
- Metal reduces and compacts Earth.
- Earth reduces and limits Fire.
- Fire reduces Wood.
- Wood absorbs Water.

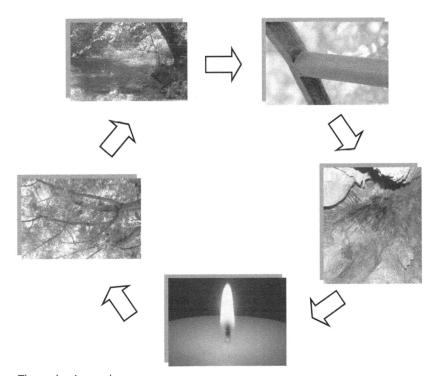

The reductive cycle.

This third set of complementary relationships—the relationships derived from the reductive cycles—are foundational principles of healing in Eastern medicine. You can see how the cycles are employed in the following case studies.

Stipple

Stipple is a 9-year-old Labrador Retriever with a weight problem. His temperament is mainly Earth. (Remember that the temperament of your pet may incorporate more than one element, but one element usually predominates.) His owners asked me to take a look at him for help with the weight problem and his general lethargy. I told the owners that we should change his protein source from a standard canned dog food to fresh venison, which is associated with Metal. Thus, in the reductive cycle, the venison will help balance out the excesses that Stipple's Earth temperament is experiencing—and help get him back to a state of physical balance and improve his energy levels.

Dagwood

Dagwood is a 7-year-old male Standard Poodle who shows signs of fear and aggression and does not take well to newcomers. Dagwood has recently been having strange behaviors arising from an excess in his Wood constitution. Because these behavior patterns have become unpredictable, his owners and I made a change to his diet to help reestablish balance and improve his behavior. Dagwood's new primary protein source is chicken, which is a Fire food that will help to reduce the excess of Wood and help the animal become more at peace with himself and his environment.

Grover

Grover, a 12-year-old male Maine Coon cat with a Water temperament, is slowly losing his muscle mass and vitality. He is also showing early signs of arthritis; he no longer goes outside to prowl his territory, preferring to lie around the house instead. Lately, his eating habits have become very finicky, and he always used to like his beef and chicken foods. I told Grover's owner that we needed to help get the yin and yang

Watch Out for Allergic Reactions to Pet Food!

For dogs, signs of a food allergy problem include persistent ear infections, belly itching, foot or limb chewing, and an itchy face. For cats, warning signs are scabs, or an itchy neck or face. See your veterinarian if your pet presents any of these symptoms. Your pet may not show adverse reactions to pet foods immediately, but you may be priming the pump for future years by exposing your pet to certain foodstuffs.

more in balance. I proposed that we change the protein in his diet to fish—salmon and tuna (in moderation), which would help him get back on track. When he's back to his old self, I'll probably suggest that he start eating some pork, which is a good place to start when trying out a new diet.

The Compromise: Feeding Whole Foods Several Days a Week

Personally, I would never feed a dog or cat something that I would not eat myself. Many of the pet owners I work with ask me, "Do I really have to cook fresh food for my pet every single day?" The answer is, of course, no. You don't have to feed your pet whole food each and every day. Your pet would probably appreciate it a great deal if you *did* prepare all the meals from scratch, of course, but strictly speaking, it's not an imperative. You and your pet can reach a reasonable compromise that involves home-prepared meals a few days a week. (My experience is that you can shift to a whole-foods diet with your pet right away, if you wish—without your pet experiencing any adverse health effects as a result of the change.)

As a responsible pet owner, you should identify a variety of foods that complement your pet's constitution and state of health. Then you should vary the diet and watch portion sizes. Talk with a veterinarian to determine the right portion size for your pet.

When incorporating whole foods into your pet's diet, don't choose pet food based on price. If you are not willing to prepare 100 percent whole foods for your pet, look for the very best off-the-shelf brands that you can work into a good rotation for your pet. Check the ingredient lists and look for foods that:

- *Avoid* artificial colors and flavors and preservatives such as ethoxyquin and BHA, as these may cause health problems in your pet.

- *Include* vitamin E and omega fatty acids.

- *List* a recognizable meat or poultry source—not a filler such as corn, millet, wheat, or rice—as the first ingredient. That protein source should complement your pet's temperament. Grains are not natural parts of your dog's or cat's diet and should not be present in the first *five* ingredients. (Those first five ingredients typically make up 85 percent of the total content of the pet food in question.)

Whatever you do, avoid foods whose meat content is supplied by meat by-products. You won't ever know what this "meat" actually is, and if you ever were to find out, you would wish you had never learned. Suffice it to say that *you* wouldn't want to eat meat by-products, which is a good-enough reason not to feed them to the pet you love.

Once you identify two or three quality brands of canned pet food that you can alternate over the course of a week, you've done your job. If you want to earn a little extra love, you can also make your pet a good home-cooked meal once a week. You can find some good ideas for recipes at www.petsynergy.com/diet.html.

The wise man should consider that health is the greatest of human blessings.
Let thy food be thy medicine.

—Hippocrates

Beyond the Pet Food Aisle

Most pet owners simply buy prepared food off the shelf for their pets . . . but there is a better way!

Suppose you're ready to take action and change what's happening in your dog's diet? Suppose you're willing to stop relying quite so heavily on prepared foods you buy at the supermarket? Suppose you're ready to start preparing a little bit more of your pet's food at home?

If you're ready to begin making this change, I think you'll find that this is a good deal easier and more convenient than you may have thought, as long as you simply follow the dietary guidelines given here. None of the ingredients I'm about to recommend is exotic or difficult to track down, and preparing the recipes will eventually take you no more than fifteen or twenty minutes.

Start small, and you can expand as you go along. When you're just getting started, consider making the preparations below for your pet one day a week and then expanding to slowly and steadily take up more and more of your dog's weekly diet.

<u>An important note:</u> *The recipes that follow are intended as single meals and a starting point for cats and dogs of medium size and build. Please check with your veterinarian to confirm the right portion size for your dog or cat.*

Remember that the diets presented in this chapter are baselines, and there can be many variations. Consult a veterinarian to make sure that this diet is best suited to your pet and that it provides the proper vitamins and minerals for him or her.

The Base Diet for Dogs

The basic recipe that follows is for a "core meal" that you can use to support good health in your dog, *regardless of your dog's primary temperament.* This diet is a good place to start for dogs of virtually all temperaments: Water, Earth, Metal, Fire, or Wood. In fact, if you don't even know your dog's primary temperament, you can still use this core recipe as a good base meal for your dog. This is for an adult dog; variations need to be made for puppies, elderly dogs, working dogs, and special-needs dogs with underlying

You are what you eat—and so is your pet!

diseases. I have included a variety of foods in the variations that follow this basic recipe; each has been composed with an eye toward overall balance.

The Basic Recipe

Here's the basic meal for dogs:

Fifteen to 20 percent of the meal should be ground turkey or beef (based on final, cooked weight). The remaining 80 to 85 percent should be divided by weight among the following ingredients; experiment with proportions over time based on your dog's preferences:

- Cooked brown rice
- Chopped, steamed broccoli
- Chopped, steamed carrots
- Cooked beets
- Cooked string beans

Before mixing, add the following:

• 1 tablespoon olive oil

   • 1 calcium supplement for humans (tablet), crushed and added to
     the mix
   • Half of a human multivitamin

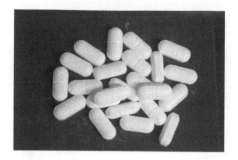

A supplementation of a vitamin and mineral tablet should be added to this diet and all other diets presented here for both dogs and cats. The supplementation of vitamins and minerals is based on your pet's size and health status, so consult your veterinarian.

Of course, you'll want to work in some changes to this recipe over time in order to add a little variety to your pet's diet. One simple way to do this is by alternating the cooked ground beef (or turkey) with cooked ground pork. You might also decide to add some sardines to the beef or pork mixture for the sake of variety. Some dogs enjoy this; others don't!

If you did only this much, you would improve the quality of your dog's diet dramatically. Giving your pet the opportunity to eat fresh foods that you cook at home is a massive improvement over a constant reliance on prepared, off-the-shelf products—typically, products that have been sitting in a warehouse for weeks or months.

Cooking and serving this basic recipe for your dog is a great place to start—and the good news is that it really doesn't take much effort. All you have to do is combine the cooked ingredients, add the crushed-up calcium supplement, mix everything together, and be ready to experiment a little. (If your dog doesn't like the mix as I've laid it out, consider experimenting with different vegetables.)

But why stop there? The basic meal I've shared with you can—and, I believe, should—serve as the foundation for expanding a regimen of healthy, home-cooked eating for your pet. It's just as easy to have a much more powerful positive impact on your dog's health and well-being by simply taking into account the animal's dominant temperament and then considering some simple variations to the core meal. I've outlined some of the many possible variations to the basic diet in the following scenarios.

In each "problem" case that appears below, I've offered a brief diagnosis of a *sample* situation where a dog's dominant temperament has been altered because of a deficiency of the dog's dominant element. In other words, the mode of behavior that you've come to know as "the way your pet typically acts" seems different, and I'm suggesting that this change in behavior has arisen because of a deficiency in your pet's primary element. In this simple case—which is certainly not the only situation you could face, but is nevertheless quite common—your goal is to *boost* your pet's temperament by incorporating the foods that are likely to support that temperament.

A word of warning about the recipes that follow: Like the core recipe, each of the meals that follow requires a certain amount of experimentation. If your pet doesn't like what you come up with, try making minor modifications or changes. I've found that swapping out one vegetable for another sometimes makes a big difference.

Remember: If your pet doesn't eat the food, it's not going to improve anything!

Diet Scenario for a Fire-Temperament Dog

This Yorkshire Terrier is a high-energy Fire dog.

- You notice that your usually active, energetic, upbeat Fire-temperament dog starts to become more withdrawn.

- You get the feeling your dog is "not himself"—and there's a reason for that. He's not acting in accordance with the dominant Fire temperament that typically influences his behavior.

- Usually he's running around, checking everything out—and now something is different. He doesn't interact with you in the way he usually does. He seems almost depressed.

Can a change in diet help to improve your Fire-temperament dog's well-being? It could, if the problem is that your dog is dealing with a Fire-element deficiency.

Try a variation where **10 percent of the meal is beef and 10 percent is ground lamb** (based on final, cooked weight). The remaining 80 percent should be divided by weight among the following, experimenting with proportions over time based on your dog's preferences:

- Cooked brown rice
- Chopped, cooked bell peppers

- Chopped, steamed carrots
- Cooked squash or pumpkin

- Cooked beets
- Cooked string beans

Before mixing, add the following:

- 1 tablespoon olive oil
- 1 calcium supplement for humans (tablet), broken up

Diet Scenario for an Earth-Temperament Dog

The calm and obedient Rhodesian Ridgeback is an Earth dog.

- You notice that your normally sociable, engaged Earth dog stops taking as much pleasure in connecting with you as he usually does. Playing with you used to be the high point of the day for your pet—but now you get the sense that it doesn't even register on his radar screen.

- You get the feeling that your dog is "not himself"—and there's a reason for that. He's not acting in accordance with the dominant Earth temperament that typically influences his behavior.

- Usually you have a strong emotional connection to your pet, and pleasing you is typically very important to him. Now he seems distant and unavailable—even lazy.

Can a change in diet help to improve your Earth-temperament dog's health and well-being? It might, if the problem is that your dog is dealing with an Earth-element deficiency.

Try a variation where **15 to 20 percent of the meal is ground pork** (based on final, cooked weight). The remaining 80 to 85 percent should be divided by weight among the following, experimenting with proportions over time based on your dog's preferences:

- Cooked brown rice
- Chopped, steamed broccoli
- Chopped, steamed carrots
- Cooked beets
- Cooked string beans

Add the following before mixing:

- 1 tablespoon olive oil
- 1 calcium supplement for humans (tablet), broken up
- 1 teaspoon of dried ginger or crushed ginger root

Diet Scenario for a Metal-Temperament Dog

This noble, disciplined Sheltie is a Metal dog.

- You notice that your normally alert, engaged, "on top of things" Metal-temperament dog doesn't seem as tuned in as usual to his environment.

- You get the feeling your dog is "not himself" because he's not acting in accordance with the dominant Metal temperament that typically influences his behavior.

- Usually, you have the sense that your dog follows everything that's going on around him and has all the angles covered; you usually feel that he's observant and eager to monitor just about everything. For some reason, though, your dog now seems disinterested in his surroundings, and is even a little dull. You suspect, too, that your dog could be experiencing digestive problems, such as constipation, in which case you should schedule a visit with your veterinarian as soon as possible.

In the meantime, though, you wonder if a change in his diet might help to improve your Metal-temperament dog's health and well-being. It could, if the problem is that your dog is dealing with a Metal-element deficiency.

Try a variation where **15 to 20 percent of the meal is ground chicken or venison** (based on final, cooked weight). The remaining 80 to 85 percent should be divided by weight among the following, experimenting with proportions over time based on your dog's preferences:

- Cooked brown rice
- Chopped, steamed broccoli
- Baked sweet potato

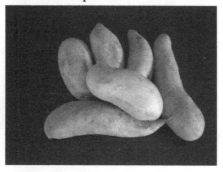

- Cooked beets
- Cooked string beans

Add the following before mixing:

- 1 tablespoon olive oil
- 1 calcium supplement for humans (tablet), broken up

Diet Scenario for a Water-Temperament Dog

- You notice that your normally playful, intelligent, and connected dog seems morose, and isn't as responsive when you try to initiate the usual activities with him.

A Water dog sitting is a classic posture, as he over-
looks his environment.

- You get the feeling your dog is "not himself"—and there's a reason for that. He's not acting in accordance with the dominant
Water temperament that typically influences his behavior.
- Usually, you have the sense that your dog depends on you for
safety, companionship, and even a sense of belonging. Now, he
doesn't seem to depend on you for much of anything. At the
same time, you may get the sense that he is feeling quite lonely—
and you may not know exactly what to do about that. You may
also notice bladder problems, in which case you should schedule
an examination with your veterinarian as soon as possible.

In the meantime, however, you wonder if a change in diet would
help improve your Water-temperament dog's health and well-being. It's
possible the problem is that your dog is dealing with a Water-element
deficiency.

Try a variation where **15 to 20 percent of the meal is ground duck
or turkey** (based on final, cooked weight). The remaining 80 to 85
percent should be divided by weight among the following, experimenting with proportions over time based on your dog's preference:

- Cooked brown rice
- Chopped, steamed broccoli
- Baked sweet potato

• Cooked beets
• Cooked string beans

Before mixing, add the following:

• 1 tablespoon olive oil
• 1 calcium supplement for humans (tablet), broken up

Diet Scenario for a Wood-Temperament Dog

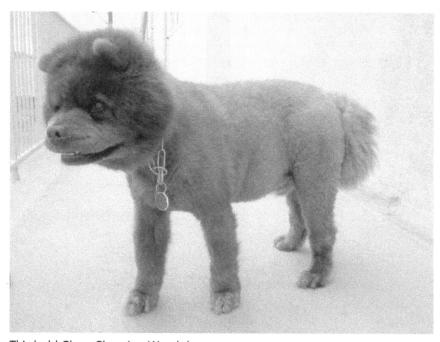

This bold Chow-Chow is a Wood dog.

• You notice that your usually bold, responsive dog starts to become more fearful, tentative, and isolated.
• You get the feeling your dog is "not himself." He's not acting in accordance with the dominant Wood temperament that typically influences his behavior.

- Usually movements and changes in the environment stimulate and interest him; he's quick to react, dynamic, and eager to make new things happen. Now, though, his own environment seems to unsettle him.

Could a change in diet help to improve your Wood-temperament dog's health and well-being? Possibly, if the problem is that your dog is dealing with a Wood-element deficiency.

Try a variation where **15 to 20 percent of the meal is chicken** (based on final, cooked weight). The remaining 80 to 85 percent should be divided by weight among the following, experimenting with proportions over time based on your dog's preferences:

- Cooked brown rice
- Cooked squash or pumpkin
- Chopped, cooked bell peppers
- Cooked beets
- Cooked string beans

Add the following ingredients before mixing:

- 1 tablespoon olive oil
- 1 calcium supplement for humans (tablet), broken up

The Base Diet for Cats

Just as I did for dogs, I created a balanced "core meal" for cats that is far preferable to feeding your cat canned or bagged food that you buy in a supermarket. I believe you'll find that the right fresh-cooked food will always be preferable to food that has been sitting around in a warehouse for long periods of time.

Cats, too, can benefit from home-cooked diets.

You can use the foundation recipe that appears below to support good health in your cat *regardless of your cat's primary temperament*. Bear in mind that cats are notoriously finicky eaters, and a little more experimentation may be in order when it comes to creating the right base dish. Once you find the right mix, though, you'll find that your cat responds to it enthusiastically!

There is a quirkiness about cats that often has to do with their personalities. Certain cats may not take well to a home-cooked diet. In some cases, I have the pet owner partially cook the meat, leaving it on the rare side, and then slowly integrate it into his or her feeding program. I also find that many cats are not too fond of vegetables. As you may know, cats are carnivores; they need protein more than anything.

Also note that cats need a vitamin and mineral supplement added to their food. The amount is based on a cat's size and health status.

Again, the recipes that follow are intended as single meals for cats of medium size and build. *Please check with your veterinarian to confirm the right portion size for your pet.*

The Base Recipe

Here's the basic meal for cats:

Twenty-five to 30 percent of the meal should be beef protein (based on final, cooked weight). *Note:* Specific cats may respond better to other proteins, such as chicken, turkey, or fish, but try beef first.

The remaining 70 to 75 percent should be divided by weight among the following; experiment with proportions over time based on your cat's preferences:

- Cooked brown rice
- Baked sweet potato

Add the following ingredients before mixing:

- 1 tablespoon olive oil
- 1 calcium supplement for humans (tablet), broken up

Now let's look at some specific situations in which you could use dietary changes to compensate for elemental deficiencies you notice in your cat.

An important note: You may also add an enzyme supplement for humans (available at health-food stores) to all these diets to help with digestion of foodstuffs. This can be in the form of probiotics (lactobacillus and Bifidio-bacterium), digestive enzymes (amylase, protease, lipase), and papaya enzymes.

Diet Scenario for a Fire-Temperament Cat

This young cat has a fiery look that exemplifies his Fire temperament.

- You notice that your usually vibrant, active cat no longer seems to want to be the center of attention. The cat exhibits less vigor and less zest for life.
- The cat seems different to you—and there's a reason. The Fire-temperament tendencies you've grown used to no longer seem as obvious.
- Usually your cat is into everything and is sometimes a bit of a nuisance. Now you've got a more subdued, withdrawn cat on your hands and you're not sure why.

Consider whether a change in diet would help to improve your Fire-temperament cat's well-being. It could, if the problem is that your cat is dealing with a Fire-element deficiency.

Try a variation to his diet where **25 to 30 percent of the meal should be chicken** (based on final, cooked weight). The remaining 70 to 75 percent should be divided by weight among the following, experimenting with proportions over time based on your cat's preferences:

- Cooked brown rice
- Baked pumpkin

Add to this before mixing:

- 1 tablespoon olive oil
- 1 calcium supplement for humans (tablet), broken up

Diet Scenario for an Earth-Temperament Cat

This Earth cat radiates calm.

- You notice that your cat, who usually loves to be with you and can't wait for you to come home, is taking less of an interest in you.
- The cat seems different to you—and there's a reason. The Earth-temperament tendencies you've grown used to no longer seem as obvious.
- Usually your cat tries to spend every waking hour with you—and maybe even every sleeping hour as well. Now the poor cat seems a lot less interested in the relationship. He seems lost somehow.

Could a change in diet help to improve your Earth-temperament cat's well-being? It might, if the problem is that your cat is dealing with an Earth-element deficiency.

Try a variation where **25 to 30 percent of the meal is beef, salmon, or sardines** (based on final, cooked weight). The remaining 70 to 75 percent should be divided by weight among the following; experiment with proportions over time based on your cat's preferences:

- Cooked brown rice
- Baked sweet potato

Before mixing, add the following:

- 1 tablespoon olive oil
- 1 calcium supplement for humans (tablet), broken up

Diet Scenario for a Metal-Temperament Cat

- You notice that your cat, who usually loves to oversee everything in the house, is not as likely to monitor the events in your home. Perhaps before, he found a place on a high perch from which to observe his domain or followed you around to see exactly what you were doing. Now he's simply not interested in what's taking place in his world.
- The cat seems different to you—and there's a reason. The Metal-temperament tendencies you've grown used to no longer seem as obvious.

This Metal cat has an ordered, disciplined look.

- Usually your cat loves to figure things out. He has always been a little aloof, and likely to consider himself the expert on everything in his world. Now, though, he seems less likely to evaluate, survey, or judge his surroundings—or the human beings who occupy them.

Can a change in diet improve your Metal-temperament cat's well-being? It's possible, if the problem is that your cat is dealing with a Metal-element deficiency.

Try a variation where **25 to 30 percent of the meal is rabbit** (based on final, cooked weight). The remaining 70 to 75 percent should be divided by weight among the following, experimenting with proportions over time based on your cat's preferences:

- Cooked brown rice
- Baked sweet potato

Before mixing, add the following ingredients:

- 1 tablespoon olive oil
- 1 calcium supplement for humans (tablet), broken up

Diet Scenario for a Water-Temperament Cat

- You notice that your cat, who has always been a creature of routine, has recently become withdrawn and has found more and more excuses to spend time by himself.

A Water cat judges his surroundings.

- The cat seems different to you—and there's a reason. The Water-temperament tendencies you've grown used to no longer seem as obvious.

- Usually your cat is loyal and depends on you to bring order to his world. Now he's retreating—everything seems to be a challenge, including spending time with him. Something's wrong, and you don't know exactly what it is, but it seems that your cat has less to rely on in his life.

Consider whether a change in diet might help to improve your Water-temperament cat's well-being. It might help, if the problem is that your cat is dealing with a Water-element deficiency. Try a variation where **25 to 30 percent of the meal is duck (available at butcher shops), white fish, or clams** (based on final, cooked weight). The remaining 70 to 75 percent should be divided by weight among the following, experimenting with proportions over time based on your cat's preference:

- Cooked brown rice
- Baked sweet potato

Add the following ingredients before mixing:

- 1 tablespoon olive oil
- 1 calcium supplement for humans (tablet), broken up

Diet Scenario for a Wood-Temperament Cat

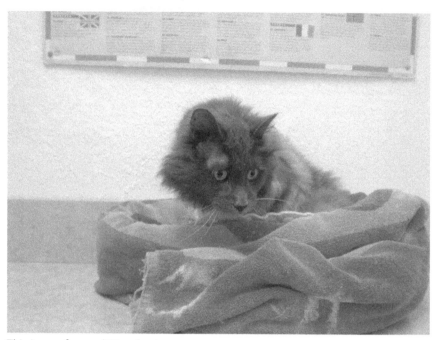

This is one focused Wood cat.

- You notice that your cat, who has always considered himself the king of the household, seems less interested in reigning over all he surveys.

- The cat seems different to you—and there's a reason. The Wood-temperament tendencies you've grown used to are no longer at the forefront.

- Usually your cat is eager to exercise his prerogatives and his authority. Now he seems curiously disengaged, which is odd behavior for a monarch.

Would a change in his diet help to improve your Wood-temperament cat's well-being? Maybe, if the problem is that your cat is dealing with a Wood-element deficiency.

Try a variation where **25 to 30 percent of the meal is chicken and/ or venison** (based on final cooked weight). The remaining 70 to 75 percent should be divided by weight among the following, experimenting with proportions over time based on your cat's preferences:

- Cooked brown rice
- Baked sweet potato

Add the following ingredients before mixing:

- 1 tablespoon olive oil
- 1 calcium supplement for humans (tablet), broken up

Some Final Thoughts

These are just a few of the most common scenarios in which a dietary change can make a positive change in your pet's health and well-being. If you decide to use processed food as part of your pet's diet, make sure you check the list of ingredients and look for the pure foods that are added to the mix. Remember that the ingredients listed first are the most plentiful; avoid foods that rely on meat and poultry by-products.

All the diets I have presented here can and should be adapted to the specific conditions of an individual pet. Work with a good veterinarian to find the right balance for your pet; you'll find a listing of holistic practitioners in the Appendix.

Chapter 7

Wholeness and Early Intervention

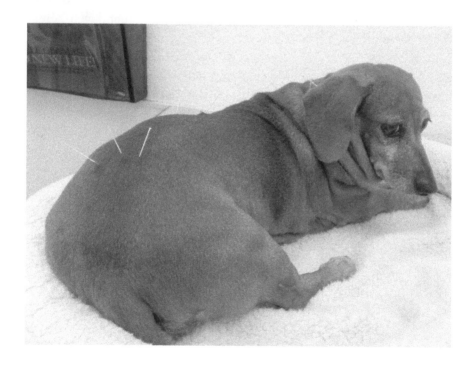

Prevention is better than cure.

—*Proverb*

What do people mean when they say they want to be "well"? Is this physical wellness, mental wellness, or the wellness that encompasses their whole lives? Most people would say that they choose the last option, but what they typically focus on is the first option.

Many people believe that if their physical state is "well," then everything else will follow suit—and they make similar assumptions about their pets. Physical well-being is part of wellness, of course, but it is not the entire picture.

The area I will discuss in this chapter is wholeness. This has to do with the way an organism survives and maintains a level of wellness as part of the "whole environment."

As an organism, you live as part of a whole environment—an integrated system, if you will—and so does your pet. For instance, your pet's organ systems function together to establish a state of equilibrium (called *homeostasis*) within the body. You feed nutritious food to your pet so that she can achieve and sustain that homeostasis within her body. Next, you exercise your pet so that she can use the nutrition to keep her body functioning properly. At this point, most pet owners feel that they've reached the borderline, the point beyond which everything is out of their control. But is it really?

The next factors to consider are the other living things in the environment that affect your pet: humans, for instance. As an owner, you have a tremendous capacity to ensure and support wellness in your pet. You can keep your pet away from danger—that much is obvious. But there's another factor that you may not always realize exists: You also exert certain kinds of energy that affect your pet.

Then there's the physical environment you share with your pet. That environment is laced with a lot of toxins that can cause stress on your pet's body. There are a lot of things that you can do about this stress. As you've learned, you can help your pet by supporting healthy *chi* flow with good nutrition; you can also help your pet by making intelligent changes in your living space. Both of these steps keep your pet integrated in a healthy way with the environment—and respect her status as part of that environment. You can also help support this idea of integration with the environment, the principle of wholeness, by making good choices for your pet in the area of early intervention. This simply means that you are willing to look at your pet's environment and lifestyle carefully and continuously, and take appropriate action to keep things in balance, even if you don't perceive anything is "wrong" with your pet.

A good example of the benefit of early intervention is the example of a small dog who lives in an urban setting. I treat many dogs who fall into this category, and I can attest that many of their owners operate under the assumption that their dogs get enough physical exercise and mental stimulation simply by moving around the house during the day. This routine is actually very likely to degrade the dog's wellness over time—but it may not present any overt physical symptoms for months or years. All living beings need to be able to grasp the good *chi* throughout the larger environment. Unfortunately, a small, closed environment limits *chi* flow. The result: stagnation. You will only notice that potential problem when you look at the animal's interaction with its environment. By taking action early to implement a better daily exercise routine, pet owners can intervene before symptoms of health problems occur—and promote a healthier, more integrated lifestyle for their pets.

Looking at the wholeness of your pet's well-being and identifying potential *chi* problems before they have adverse effects is, I believe, the key to unlocking the mystery of true wellness for the animal in your life. In this chapter, you'll read about some cases from my practice that will help you learn why it's so important to intervene early to change routines that may not be supporting your pet's health. You will also see some of the dangers of not intervening early, and you'll learn why you must sometimes go out of the mainstream to make changes to your shared lifestyle—changes that support wholeness and are in the best interests of you and your pet.

> *In a disordered mind, as in a disordered body, soundness of health is impossible.*
>
> —Cicero

Bergeron

Bergeron was an energetic, overweight adult Sheltie who made a habit of jumping on and off the bed of his owner, Lisa. "It used to be part of his routine," Lisa told me. "He just loved jumping from the floor to the bed and from the bed to the floor. Usually he was doing it to follow me somewhere. For a couple of months, though, he seemed to be jumping in a funny way, kind of with a twinge."

Bergeron had serious back problems.

The act of jumping may have been an enjoyable part of Bergeron's routine, but apparently the dog had executed too many "funny" jumps. On one of those jumps, he landed badly and injured—or, to be more accurate, *reinjured*—his back. Bergeron had probably sustained other minor injuries to his back over the years. Lisa took him to his regular veterinarian who gave him his yearly checkup and made sure that his vaccinations were up-to-date. The veterinarian examined Bergeron closely and saw that he was not able to move his back legs in order to support himself, much less walk. He took bloodwork and X-rays in order to locate the problem. The function of Bergeron's rear legs was lost, although he still had feeling in his rear legs.

Tests showed that Bergeron had slipped a disc in his back. The veterinarian prescribed a series of medications and hospitalized him for a few days, but there was no improvement.

The veterinarian gave Lisa the option of seeing an animal neurologist and possibly arranging surgery for Bergeron. Unfortunately, this path was quite expensive—and far out of Lisa's reach financially. What's more, there was no guarantee that Bergeron would be able to walk after undergoing the procedure. The only other option, according to the veterinarian, was to put Bergeron down.

For a few days, Lisa put off the decision about what to do next. She was bothered by the vet's quick conclusion that there was "nothing to be done" other than surgery. This is the point at which many pet owners seek me out: after they've been told by a conventionally trained veterinarian that the most intelligent, responsible, and "ethical" course of action is to order the death of their pet. For many people, this course of action feels strange, difficult, and even selfish. I often wonder how many pet owners would seek out alternative treatments for their pets if they knew what actually happened when pet owners sought second opinions after getting advice to put their pets to sleep. There have been remarkable success stories, where the animals have made dramatic improvements. They seem miraculous to many pet owners, but in fact what is happening is that the practitioner is trying to move the body into a more balanced state and establish a more profound harmony with the environment.

Sometimes, of course, an animal is in so much pain that a carefully considered decision to end the pet's life really is the right course of action. Veterinarians look at some diseases, like cancer, and know that the pet is in anguish and that it is time for her to depart. Sometimes, though, there are other options. Lisa could see that Bergeron was dragging his rear and falling over, but she could also clearly see that there was no quitting in his eyes. No matter how hard it was for him to get around, he would get there. Lisa set her mind straight and investigated other modes of potential treatment. She asked me for a second opinion.

I did a thorough exam and looked over Bergeron's test results; I, too, concluded that there was most likely a disc that had slipped. At this point, Bergeron still had sensitivity in his rear legs but could not stand or walk. I sat down with Lisa and got an in-depth history. Then I shared my thoughts with her.

In brief, Bergeron was predominantly an Earth-type, and what had occurred here was an imbalance or stagnation in the system that manifested itself with a slipped disc. What did his Earth constitution have to do with this? First of all, as you recall, Earth pets love to do everything with their owners. Also, Earth pets are relaxed, poised, and sometimes more sedentary. This was a pet who had the potential to put on weight . . . and that he did. This weight gain led to an extra load on his body, and there came a point when Bergeron's body could no longer handle the stress. Then a disc ruptured.

We set up Bergeron with a more nutritious diet to help his body use the nutrients better and of course to help him lose weight. We changed the spot where Bergeron slept, moving his bed to a more vibrant part of the house so that some of the laziness that had been present did not take its toll and cause an ongoing stagnation of energy. We also gave him a set of acupuncture treatments, which helped to relieve the pain and decreased both muscle spasms and inflammation. Within three days, the dog was walking again. The effects of the diet were not as immediate as those of the acupuncture, but we were able to use both treatments to set him on a path of healing.

This is a classic example of looking at the body and the environment as a whole: We made changes to Bergeron's body *and* his environment.

Lisa makes a point of helping Bergeron get on and off high surfaces now because once an animal has a slipped disc, that animal is at risk for future back problems. Just as a human being would, ideally, avoid playing tackle football after a problem with a slipped disc, a dog, too, needs to be careful.

Lessons from Bergeron's Story

I did not tell you Bergeron's story because I think that every veterinarian who recommends that a dog or cat be euthanized is acting irresponsibly. That's certainly not true! There are two very different lessons that I want you to draw from Bergeron's story: one for pet owners and the other for veterinarians.

First and foremost, seemingly minor changes in a pet's behavior, lifestyle, physical structure, and ability are the owner's responsibility to notice and bring to the attention of qualified medical personnel. This should happen sooner rather than later. When Lisa noticed that Bergeron's jumps had become "funny" with a new "twinge," she should have immediately brought the dog to her veterinarian for an examination.

The other lesson you can draw from Bergeron's experience is connected to the first lesson. When pet owners ignore a problem with their pets, the pets sometimes don't get examined until after the problem has moved beyond the traditional experience base of Western medicine.

That may lead some—not all, but some—veterinarians to declare, prematurely, that there is nothing to be done. I think veterinarians need to be open to other modalities in order to do what we take an oath to do: serve and help animals and relieve them of undue suffering. This does not always mean euthanasia.

Cadbury

Cadbury's system was out of balance, and he had problems with renal disease.

The same two critical lessons—the necessity for prompt action on the part of the pet owner and a willingness to look at different ways of treating the animal—show up in Cadbury's story. Fortunately, I was able to work with this cat's owners and help bring about a good outcome, even though I examined Cadbury later than I would have liked.

Cadbury was an orange mixed-breed cat who was having problems his owners could not explain, including his inability to finish his moist food. The owners brought him to me with a laundry list of problems. After I took a history and did a complete physical exam incorporating both Eastern and Western methodologies, I determined that Cadbury had the following problems:

- He was drinking a lot of water.
- His appetite had decreased.
- He had weight loss, which made the bones of his spine protrude.
- His kidneys were small.
- His coat was unkempt.

The next step was to take bloodwork, do a urinalysis, and do some X-rays. The diagnosis was kidney failure.

The situation was pretty grim. When I shared the test results with Cadbury's owners, they told *me* that the time had come to consider putting the cat down! That option was certainly something we could have looked at, but I wanted to try to take this case in a different direction.

Cadbury had more medical options than his owners realized.

I explained to Cadbury's owners that we still had a few options to consider before we started thinking about ending the cat's life. They heard me out and we agreed on a course of treatment that incorporated both Eastern and Western therapies.

Cadbury was a Water cat. He was also an "indoor and outdoor" cat and could not be kept locked up for long periods. When let out, he would always sit on the fence and almost look like a king lording over his grounds. Cadbury's symptoms matched up with the typical problems that can occur with Water cats when in crisis, such as weight loss, arthritis, and excess water consumption. I worked out a plan with the owners to put him on a nutritional program that would get him to start taking in more quality protein. Of course, for cats their diet is the hardest thing to adjust because of their individualized nuances and behavioral patterns.

The next treatment, taken from the Western world, was to give him daily fluids under the skin in order to help him with hydration. We also started herbal treatments, but these needed to be taken slowly because of Cadbury's dissatisfaction with the taste. Minor changes in the environment where Cadbury spent most of his time helped to support nourishment and vibrant energy. Taken together, the changes in the treatments, the eating regimen, and the physical space ended up giving Cadbury two more quality years of life with his owners!

Lessons from Cadbury's Story

Even today, I can't help but wonder whether we might have been able to win even more time for Cadbury if I'd gotten to see him earlier. Faced with the same situation again, I know his owners would have brought him in for an examination before the symptoms became as severe as they did.

Just as a good M.D. does when treating a human being, a good veterinarian will look for reasons to prolong quality years of life when evaluating an animal patient. For some reason—a reason I suspect may have something to do with less-than-ideal communication between pet owner and veterinarian—a very different cycle sometimes unfolds when a pet's health and well-being are at issue. As Cadbury's owners' reaction suggests, people sometimes feel that they are at a dead end when something major occurs in their pets. They are looking at the quality of their lives, and also in the backs of their minds, they conclude that their pets do not have a lot of time to spend with them. They make assumptions, sometimes without all the relevant facts at hand.

The other lesson has to do with the importance of looking at your pet in combination with its temperament and its environment as a whole. Cadbury, an aloof Water cat, always kept himself at a distance. Because of his personality, he needed more personal attention, not less. Had his owners noticed the changes a little earlier, his potentially life-threatening problems could have been detected before they became *actual* life-threatening problems.

Let me be very clear here: I am not saying that problems arise because pet owners or veterinarians are somehow morally deficient. It's because pet owners and veterinarians often don't *communicate* frequent-ly enough, or in enough detail, before minor problems escalate into major crises. As a result, some (and again, not all) people allow them-selves to get painted into a corner. They face a stark and painful choice: to take heroic (and often expensive) measures or to end the pet's life. To me, the truly astonishing thing is that, after having faced this terrible choice—and, of course, in a perfect world no pet owner would face it even once—they may actually become habituated to it. By the time they encounter a serious health problem that affects a second, third, fourth, or fifth pet, they may be thinking twice whether the options that are set before them would make their pet healthy again even though there are still plenty of good reasons to prolong that life and plenty of strategies for doing so. If you *can* keep your pet from getting life-threatening diseases by taking a more proactive approach, then shouldn't you?

Of course, ending a pet's life prematurely is a mistake. I don't know exactly why it happens, but I know that it does. One possible reason is that pet owners who have experienced the difficulty of seeing a pet go through physical pain are in no hurry to repeat that experience. Perhaps that's an understandable response, but given that every animal's condi-tion deserves to be evaluated independently (just as every human being's does), the pet's vitality and quality of life must be considered closely, and all the options must be weighed carefully.

When you make a mistake, don't look back at it long. Take the reason of the thing into your mind and then look forward. Mistakes are lessons of wisdom. The past cannot be changed. The future is yet in your power.

—Hugh White, nineteenth-century U.S. politician

Samantha

Samantha showed great courage in battling cancer.

The third story I want to share with you illustrates, in a particularly vivid and painful way, the importance of not allowing yourself to get painted into a corner by circumstances. You always want to leave yourself and your pet with plenty of options, as this story illustrates. It's a story I will never forget, and one I hope you'll never forget, either.

Samantha was a 12-year-old mixed-breed dog who had grown up with her owners, Max and Joanne. When Samantha's energy waned and her appetite started to diminish, Max and Joanne explained it by telling themselves that the dog was "just getting old" and thus did not have the same energy or desire for food that she'd had in years past.

Weeks passed, and then the owners started to worry because Samantha suddenly seemed to lose a lot of weight. They took her to their veterinarian, who diagnosed Samantha as having intestinal problems. He prescribed medications to help her intestinal problems and put her on a new prescription diet. He asked her owners to check back in a few weeks.

On her next visit, Samantha seemed to feel and look a little bit better, so the veterinarian continued the medication and prescription diet and asked the owners to return in another few weeks. They did, but by that point, Samantha's condition had begun to deteriorate again. The vet continued with an enhanced treatment and added steroids to the mix.

Weeks went by, and Samantha continued to wax and wane. Unfortunately, her condition worsened and she seemed to hit a new low. Months after the veterinarian had begun his treatment, he did an ultrasound and saw that a huge tumor had developed on Samantha's intestine. He advised her owners that it was time to have Samantha put down.

This discussion was truly heartbreaking because Max, Joanne, and their three children considered Samantha to be a part of the family. None of their kids could remember a time when Samantha had not been a member of the household. Distraught, they talked to another veterinarian—but he offered the same seemingly unthinkable recommendation: to put her to sleep. The family concluded that there simply had to be another option. They started asking friends and relatives for ideas for alternative treatment. Eventually, an in-law suggested that they contact me.

When I saw Samantha's nearly skeletal frame and heard her medical history, my heart broke, too. I knew that if I had been brought in earlier, when the changes in behavior and appetite had begun to manifest themselves, I might have been able to take steps to help Samantha. I probably could have found a way to help support her situation with alternative medicine in conjunction with mainstream methods. This treatment may have included surgery to remove the tumor and then the use of Eastern techniques to help her waning system become more balanced. As it was, I instituted a series of herbal treatments. They extended Samantha's life by a few months. This was the best I could do to help her at that point. I felt terrible for the entire family.

Health is a state of complete harmony of the body, mind and spirit.
When one is free from physical disabilities and mental distractions,
the gates of the soul open.

—B. K. S. Iyengar

Lessons from Samantha's Story

Max and Joanne thought of Samantha as a member of the family, but, unfortunately, they took the advice to wait and see how conventional therapy panned out. The minute Max and Joanne noticed something unusual about Samantha's behavior and energy level, they could have begun doing exactly what they would have done if they'd noticed sudden changes in behavior and energy that indicated a change in their children's health and well-being: called a doctor!

Instead, they delayed getting her initial care and then they took the advice of their family veterinarian when he initiated treatment. There is nothing wrong with seeing and starting treatment with your veterinarian. But I do think you need to notice when that treatment isn't getting you anywhere. In this case, the veterinarian was not helping Samantha to get better.

I realize that it's very difficult for an owner to know whom to trust when a pet's life is at stake. I also know that, in this case, Samantha was losing precious time—time that she did not have. The options presented to her owners should have included alternative approaches for her care, and her owners should have intervened earlier than they did. Had they begun the whole discussion earlier, they could have insisted on seeing and evaluating those options so that they could have gotten a fuller picture of her whole situation, not just one tiny corner of it. The lack of emphasis on early detection and intervention is a major gap in the care of pets—a gap I am trying to fill with my practice and with this book. The later you begin treating a problem, the harder it is to think about wholeness and the temperament of a given animal. When medical intervention occurs too late, your animal suffers.

Sickness is the vengeance of nature for the violation of her laws.

—*Charles Simmons*

Beyond Late Diagnosis and Early Euthanasia

I believe that a cycle of late intervention, late diagnosis, and early euthanasia plagues many aspects of contemporary veterinary medicine.

Fortunately, there are six simple things you can do to make sure that this cycle does not adversely affect your pet:

1. **Don't wait until you are placed in a reactive state to call your veterinarian.** Make sure your pet gets a checkup once a year. Your pet's condition changes all the time. If you and your veterinarian are not discussing the best ways to adapt to the changes that have taken place over the past twelve months, you may be setting up yourself for future problems.

2. **Build a relationship with an alternative practitioner *and* a conventional practitioner—or, even better, someone who integrates both traditions.** Visit that practitioner once a year. See the Appendix for a list of alternative practitioners (organized by state).

3. **Pay attention!** Make an honest effort to notice changes in your pet's appetite, behavior, energy level, and so on. As you saw in chapter 2, "Evaluating Pet Wellness through Purposeful Petting," your goal should be to make the time you spend interacting with your pet "aware time."

4. **When you do notice a change, don't ignore it or chalk it up to the idea that your pet is getting older.** That's all the more reason to seek medical attention immediately!

5. **In evaluating any change in your pet's behavior or activity, get the best assessments you can from both Western and Eastern veterinary traditions.**

6. **Ask your veterinarian questions when he or she recommends a course of treatment.** You have a right to ask questions, and you have a right to decide for yourself when the answers you get are unacceptable. If your veterinarian won't communicate with you about a given course of treatment or about alternatives to that treatment, find another practitioner. Again, the alternative practitioners listed in the Appendix are a good place to start.

If you follow these six steps, you'll be able to support the kind of wellness that encompasses your whole pet's life and the environment in which your pet lives. You'll give yourself—and your pet—more options, and you'll be less likely to be painted into a corner by a sudden emergency. You'll be more likely to spot and resolve problems with your pet before they become life-threatening situations. And, of course, you'll enjoy more quality time with him or her.

Chapter 8

Your Fire Pet

A classic Fire dog.

By this point, you know that your pet is likely to have one of five dominant temperaments:

1. Fire

2. Earth

3. Metal

4. Water

5. Wood

In this chapter, we'll look more closely at Fire pets; subsequent chapters will examine each of the other four temperaments. To help you make sense of these chapters, however, I must share a few basic ideas with you.

First and foremost, a word about the classifications themselves is in order. The five-element theory supporting these five temperaments has become a major part of my practice. It helps me to identify problems that may occur with pets with distinct personalities. Learning this theory can help you, too. This five-element theory is not just for veterinarians; it is something that all pet owners can become more familiar with and use to understand their pets more fully. It is part of the "who" of your animal's identity, a tool you can and should use regularly to monitor your pet's changing conditions. You can also use this tool to get some perspective on the way your pet acts. This is important because people often impart "human" motives to animal behaviors that they don't fully understand. (Many pet owners assume, for instance, that an upbeat Fire pet who whimpers must be signaling pain or discomfort; in fact, this is often a signal the animal uses to draw attention to something important that is happening in his world.)

This is the Chinese character for Fire.

Second, a dominant temperament is likely to present itself in any given pet, but it won't necessarily be the only elemental temperament of a pet. Pets often exhibit *both* a dominant and a secondary temperament within the five-element system.

A third point that will help you get a better sense of the information in this and subsequent chapters is something many pet owners are already familiar with: Most pets age faster than their human owners. There are exceptions to this—reptiles, birds, and other animals—but for most pet owners, and certainly for owners of cats and dogs, the reality is that you will watch your pet's life cycle play out before you. It's almost as though your pet is presenting a preview of coming attractions concerning your own aging process and your own mortality. This dynamic of accelerated change means, among other things, that the composition and temperament of your pet can sometimes change before your eyes— and may happen faster than you realize. As a pet owner, you will need to make adjustments in your own pet's routine in order to help optimize his health and well-being, based on where your pet is in his life cycle, and what temperamental changes he is undergoing within the five-element system.

I believe that the five-element theory may be the most understandable and accessible component of Eastern wellness philosophy for pet owners who are only familiar with Western veterinary traditions. The five-element theory gives you a better idea about what your pet is doing, how he feels, and, ultimately, what kind of life transitions he is making.

Over the next five chapters, I'll use the five-element system to take a closer look at some of the health challenges faced by particular pets with particular dominant temperaments. You'll also learn about some of the ways the pet owners with whom I've worked have been able to restore balance to their pets' lives, and their own, using principles drawn from Eastern medicine. Let me emphasize that what I'll be discussing in these next chapters is the *dominant* temperament in a given pet. For simplicity's sake, I've chosen examples and treatment strategies in these chapters that align with one of the five temperaments. Please remember, too, that an animal's dominant temperament may change over time.

By the time you've finished reading this part of the book, you should have a good sense of your own pet's dominant temperament, and you should be able to have a meaningful discussion with your veterinarian about supporting your pet's health and well-being with various forms of alternative care that are likely to complement Western veterinary medicine.

Note: The examples I am using in this and subsequent chapters relate to dogs and cats, but can easily be extrapolated to other pets.

Characteristics of a Fire Pet

Fire animals are routinely upbeat and are easily enthused. They want to make you happy. Physical movement and interaction with humans and animals constitute a big part of their "vocabulary." (The table lists the characteristics, organs, and *feng shui* color associated with Fire-temperament pets.)

When this pet is in a balanced state of health, the animal is likely to be perceived as peppy, positive, and energetic. A common challenge for owners, especially where younger animals are concerned, is the problem of the pet having too much physical energy to devote to the relationship! Interestingly, people who have dominant Fire temperaments may not be attracted to these types of pets; people who are more easygoing may make the happiest owners of these pets. The latter may be more tolerant of Fire behavior in animals, or more appreciative of the ample life energy a Fire pet brings to the living environment.

Some owners perceive the Fire pet as having too much energy, but what is really going on is that this pet is radiating all that energy as an expression of happiness and positive emotion, and is waiting for its owner to welcome this energy. Fire pets become very attached to their owners and may seem at times to have separation anxiety when the owner has to go somewhere. They may also seem disobedient; in many of these situations, the animal is simply focusing with intensity on a particular distraction in its world. Resolve the distraction, and the disobedience problem disappears.

The Fire-temperament animal is likely to be poking, prodding, exploring, and interacting with the physical world that surrounds it. Like all creatures, Fire pets are likely to have periods of activity alternating with periods of inactivity—but the periods of activity for these animals may be perceived as intense by any human who happens to be in the neighborhood.

Fire animals are associated with the internal organs of the heart and small intestines. These pets may have health issues that arise from the heart: irregular heartbeats, perhaps, or other heart-related conditions. They may also develop issues associated with the small intestine, such as diarrhea, vomiting, and weight loss. Since these are the organ systems that are closely related to the Fire temperament, you want to keep an eye out for these signs whenever an imbalance first appears within the pet's system.

Element	Personality Traits	Disposition	Favorite Activities	Associated Organs	*Feng Shui* Color
Fire	Lively, charismatic, vocal, aware, enthusiastic, devoted, alert	Attentive, active	Running, interacting with others, performing obedience exercises, focus of attention	Small intestine, heart	Red

There is a circadian clock that is also affiliated with the organ system and there is a time of day when these organs are functioning optimally. Thousands of years ago, practitioners studied this clock and were able to map out when during the day the *chi* within each organ system flowed at its peak. Below is the clock that correlates to each organ system.

As you can see from the accompanying figure, the time of day that the heart is at full function is likely to be between 11:00 a.m. and 1:00 p.m. The optimal time for the small intestine is between 1:00 and 3:00 p.m.

The circadian clock is associated with organ systems.

Sometimes, when there are imbalances within the Fire composition, you will see signs of problems within these organ systems occurring at these times. On the other hand, when everything is in balance, you may see the Fire pet feeling very good at these times, and even walking with a particularly sprightly and spunky step.

You Probably Have a Fire-Temperament Dog If . . .

- Your dog is usually happy, outgoing, and energetic.
- Your dog is rambunctious and enjoys running around the house.
- Your dog is energetic and prone to initiate a display of physical affection toward you or others by jumping, running, or otherwise engaging with you physically.
- Your dog is deeply devoted to you and your family.

You Probably Have a Fire-Temperament Cat If . . .

- Your cat is playful and almost always responsive to overtures from you to engage in physical play.
- Your cat jumps and leaps any time it is looking for attention.
- Your cat is always looking for ways to be right in your face by finding spots near you on your couch, counter, or other high places.
- Your cat is eager to express physical affection, and does so vigorously.

Wanda

Wanda was a Jack Russell Terrier with a strong Fire temperament. James, her owner, reported that Wanda always seemed happy. She was always willing to please, and on any given day she was likely to be jumping

Wanda needed to calm her Fire excess to be more balanced.

around James's home. There were a lot of wild animals in the backyard, and they drew Wanda's attention on a regular basis.

James lived on a very busy street where kids were often playing. Watching the kids would get Wanda all excited and wound up. As the years progressed, Wanda seemed to become more and more "hyper." She was almost too much for James to handle sometimes.

"I still loved taking her out for walks," James told me, "but it became more and more of a job. She just couldn't seem to settle down. She became more and more uneasy, even though I would walk her whenever she seemed to want to go for a walk." James even started to attend agility classes with Wanda so he could spend more time with her and help her burn off the excess energy.

Then one day, while James and Wanda were out on a walk, he noticed a problem: a change in Wanda's walk.

"She just started to walk oddly, and it got worse and worse. Eventually it was like she was missing a step everywhere we went on our walks. She wasn't holding herself the way she usually did. Something was wrong. It didn't seem like she had good control in her legs."

James called me; I examined Wanda and found that she had a lesion on the neck. It wasn't just her neck, though. Everything was tense, and she was experiencing what seemed like serious muscle spasms. This was what was affecting her legs and her walk; the muscles in her neck were very, very tense, and they needed to relax. (The fact that Wanda was a Fire-temperament dog did not, of course, mean that she could *only* experience physical problems with the heart or small intestine. It just meant that she was, and indeed still is, particularly vulnerable to such problems.)

Wanda was out of balance; she started to build up stagnation in certain parts of her body. Her Fire temperament had led her to a situation where there was an excess of Fire. Fixing that imbalance wasn't something that James could have done on his own.

Wanda's constant energy, physical activity, and "jumpiness" had escalated into a serious physical problem. My job was to get her to calm down, which is another way of saying that my job was to bring her temperament back into balance. Another veterinarian might have prescribed a host of drugs to relax the muscles, but I wanted to learn a little more about Wanda before I settled on any course of treatment.

I talked with James in depth about Wanda's daily activity pattern. The more I learned, the more convinced I became that the problems she was experiencing were connected to an activity-related imbalance that had manifested in the neck.

The treatment here was to calm the Fire temperament and also open up the meridians (or pathways) in the body to help alleviate the stagnation. This problem had been rooted in the "jumpy" behavior that was so typical of dogs with pronounced Fire temperaments.

During the day, whenever James went to work, Wanda had always frequented the front room. The apartment had a series of beautiful picture windows, and James was in the habit of leaving the curtains open so that Wanda could see outside during the day. It was a good instinct, but it had an unfortunate outcome. She'd see people walk past—notably people like the gardener and the mail carrier—and then start running around and barking. The more people she saw during the day, the more aggravated she got. She'd run from window to window, get more and more worked up, and aggravate herself.

Instead of prescribing muscle relaxants, I asked James to close the curtains, change Wanda's location during the day, change her feeding spot, and spend more time with her if possible. I also began a program of acupuncture therapy to help restore the free flow of meridians in her body. Within two weeks, her life—and James's life—was back in balance. Wanda's spasms had ceased, and her walks with James had become the enjoyable highlights of the week that they had once been. It isn't quite accurate to say that Wanda became a quiet dog . . . but it is fair to say that she was a good deal happier.

More Traits of Fire Pets

Even in periods of balance and normalcy, Fire dogs and cats can be very lively and vocal. They are charismatic and take on a personality that is very curious. They can be a lot of fun, and may play for extended periods of time, especially with their owners. For example, in Wanda's case, she was willing to take on the agility class because she became very focused and loved to interact and "play" with her owner.

Fire animals that have excess Fire in their composition can become overly excitable—too easily upset, too aggressive, and too eager to please. Sometimes they nip at their owners, which is not to be confused with the nipping behavior of puppies. This behavior is a sign that something is out of balance. Fire pets who have Fire in excess can also be anxious and show signs of compulsiveness and hypersensitivity to changes within their environment. They may startle easily and get extremely agitated over small things. They can be very sensitive to petting and being picked up. Your pet may have always been used to brushing or being picked up but now is very hesitant to be brushed or picked up at all. This is a dramatic change and she no longer seeks this interaction.

Fire animals that have deficiencies may tire easily on walks. They seem lifeless at times and lack that fiery drive that you like about them. They may start to have a heart *arrhythmia* (irregular heartbeat) that can manifest as lethargy or disengagement.

Fire pets sometimes have difficulty with things that are meant to bring order to their lives. Many have big difficulties with training because training is usually built around a set of boundaries. These pets do not like boundaries, and are particularly resistant to training by someone other than the owner, from whom they will require constant reinforcement.

Even in the presence of their owners, Fire pets are bold and will test the boundaries of other animals or people. They may have difficulty adapting to things that are new and unusual to them, and are likely to be skeptical about, or even feel threatened by, new environments and people. They do not like to be out of control. A Fire cat may endure significant pain and discomfort to defend an outdoor territory. Fire pets have the most difficulty during warm-to-hot weather changes, and as a general rule do not like the summer months. Hot foods can aggravate their system. The accumulation of heat in their systems can take them out of balance, leading to problems such as grouchiness and erratic, unpredictable behavior, accompanied by changes in sleeping and eating patterns.

Fire-temperament animals are very energetic—sometimes too energetic for their own good. Here are some tips for managing your Fire pet:

- Avoid feeding him in the kitchen (this is considered a fiery place in the household).
- Give him a special place to eat and rest that is usually calmer than the rest of the house—say, the dining room.
- If you must leave your Fire pet alone during the day, do your best to limit visual or auditory exposure to unfamiliar people and animals (for example, keep the curtains closed).

Chapter 9

Your Earth Pet

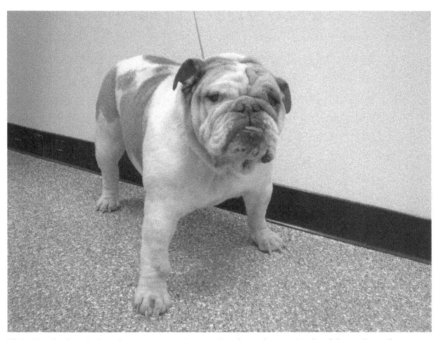

This Earth dog is low-key, supportive, poised, and seemingly able to handle anything that comes its way.

From the high-energy Fire temperament we move to the more subdued and serene Earth temperament.

The earth, of course, is all around you. It is everywhere you look. From the mountains to the lush grassy hills, the earth is a support matrix for all dependent life. The earth is ever-present, changing as the seasons change to support the varying forms of life . . . and also the inevitable process of death.

The earth is like a sponge: It receives everything. Within its embrace it contains fluids, such as rain, and solids, such as plant life. It nourishes plants and helps them produce their fruit. It also takes plants that are dead and transforms them into nutrients that will help new life develop.

The earth is very soothing. The earth is at ease with itself, so it is able to help others become more stable. You feel it when you lie on the ground with your pet: Connecting with the solidity and serenity of the earth seems to stabilize your life, somehow, if only briefly, and just like you, your pet seems to get some stability from the simple act of lying on the ground.

The earth is always changing to help and benefit other life forms; it is capable of continuing its existence under virtually any extreme but gets its power from being the stable matrix one is seeking out.

A pet whose dominant temperament is Earth evokes all of these qualities, too. This is the pet that is low key, supportive, poised, and seemingly able to handle anything that comes its way. This pet seems laid-back and doesn't appear to have a mean bone in its body. Earth pets are eager to please and very adaptable to whatever their owner is doing; they never seem to take offense at any course of action because they truly feel that their owner is always looking out for them. A Labrador Retriever with an Earth constitution makes a truly great hunting dog because she knows that her owners will be very good to her.

The Earth temperament is associated with the stomach and the spleen/pancreas. Accordingly, when there is a disturbance

This is the Chinese character for Earth.

with the balance within the Earth pet, the pet may exhibit signs of vomiting or diarrhea. The spleen and pancreas are involved in the processing of food; the stomach is like a big vat that is preparing the foodstuffs to be digested and absorbed. The Earth pet who is out of balance may have flareups between 7:00 and 9:00 a.m. with the stomach and 9:00 and 11:00 a.m. with the spleen/pancreas. It is important to remember this because you may see your Earth pet vomit every morning before meals. This can be an early sign that there is an imbalance.

*Once again, for the sake of clarity, I'm focusing on the traits associated with **primary** temperaments in this part of the book.*

Characteristics of an Earth Pet

Earth animals are not very excitable; their outlook on existence might be described as "Life is good." Life as it presents itself is so enjoyable, in fact, that many Earth pets appear to excel at just hanging around. (The accompanying table lists the characteristics, organs, and *feng shui* color associated with Earth-temperament pets.)

Very occasionally, events will stimulate an Earth pet to get up and investigate what just happened, but for the most part, they're content to avoid rousing themselves unless they absolutely have to. Most of the time, it takes a pretty big emergency to inspire action from these pets.

Sometimes pet owners get used to this laid-back attitude and assume that they just don't need to interact much with their Earth pets. This is an unfortunate attitude because without interaction from the owner the Earth pet's cycle of inactivity can often perpetuate itself in an unhealthy way. Imbalances can become more pronounced, and the pet can become lethargic and withdrawn—and perhaps even come to feel neglected. I sometimes advise owners of Earth pets to make sure their animals get regular exposure to an area of the house that is high-energy, boisterous, and full of activity, so the pets can benefit from interacting with other members of the household. If pet owners don't take this step of consciously involving their pets in the activities of the home, some Earth pets are likely to end up becoming more and more sluggish over time.

Element	Personality Traits	Disposition	Favorite Activities	Associated Organs	*Feng Shui* Color
Earth	Supportive, relaxed, stable, sociable, poised, attentive	Gentle and calm	Wants to do everything with her owner and activities are conducive to making her owner happy	Spleen/pancreas and stomach	Yellow

You Probably Have an Earth-Temperament Dog If . . .

- Your dog is laid-back—and likes it that way.
- Your dog doesn't get too worked up about much of anything, and seems to be happy to take life as it comes.
- Your dog is relaxed most of the time, enjoying the feeling of being near the energy and interaction in the household, but not necessarily participating in the activities unless a special situation arises.

You Probably Have an Earth-Temperament Cat If . . .

- Your cat spends most of the day lounging. Someone who didn't know your cat well might use the word *lazy*, but you know better. This animal likes to make careful, well-considered investments when it comes to things like time, attention, and movement.
- Your cat spends large amounts of time watching over its environment.

- Your cat is affectionate enough, but unlikely to greet you energetically when you come home. He or she prefers to be approached and petted.

Spoony

Janice started to notice that Spoony, her big, male Labrador Retriever, was slowing down at around 3 years of age. She had read that this was about the time when Labradors tend to calm down a bit. That's exactly what happens in this breed: Labrador Retrievers begin to get a little bit slower and more sedate after about 3 years of age. That high-energy puppy phase does not last forever, but these dogs do need to interact with people, even if that means giving them a little encouragement to do so from time to time!

Unfortunately, when Janice noticed Spoony starting to slow down, she assumed that he simply didn't need to exercise anymore; she told herself that this new inactivity was simply "part of the dog's life cycle."

Spoony's eating patterns had to be brought back into balance.

As a result, she would rarely try to engage Spoony. Sometimes, on the weekends, she would pull out the ball and start throwing it around, trying to get Spoony to show some kind of interest in the familiar game of fetch. Sometimes he did; sometimes he didn't. Most of the time, Spoony just kind of laid around.

Whenever the dog felt like varying his routine a little bit, he ate. In fact, he had a voracious appetite, and Janice had never thought much about limiting his food intake. Just as she had assumed that older Labs naturally did not want much in the way of interaction with humans, she assumed that they must eat more as they got older.

Not surprisingly, Spoony's weight problem got worse and worse, until eventually, the weight issue got Janice's attention and she started thinking about getting her dog out for more exercise. When Janice tried to take Spoony on a walk, however, she found that he wouldn't want to go very far. That's when she reached out to me and asked me to examine her dog and suggest a course of treatment for obesity.

As usual, I talked through the owner's history with the pet. We changed Spoony's diet, and we found ways to increase his playtime by scheduling specific periods when he would interact with Janice each and every day. We also made sure that Spoony spent more time in a more active part of the house—by moving his bed from Janice's bedroom to the family room. (Just buying another pet bed would not have been a good solution because the goal was to change where the dog was sleeping at all times.)

Now Spoony's doing great. He's lost a lot of excess weight, he's much more active, and he seems a lot more content.

Carlton

Carlton was a 2-year-old domestic longhaired cat who was found abandoned at 4 weeks of age. Ben, his owner, began his relationship with Carlton by bottle-feeding him, and always gave him as much as he wanted at all feedings.

Carlton matured and grew. By age 1, he started to look very big and weighed in at 10 pounds. By 18 months he was 15 pounds; by the age of 2 he was 19 pounds.

Changes to Carlton's diet and more exercise helped him to lose a lot of excess weight and improved his energy level.

When Ben brought Carlton in to see me for a checkup, he thought Carlton was "just a big cat." I explained to him that Carlton was a dangerously *overweight* cat who could be facing a whole host of medical problems if we didn't do something.

I came to find out that Carlton was fed half a can of food in the morning and half a can of food in the evening—and that his bowl was kept full with kibble at all times. He always wanted to be with Ben and sometimes would cry loudly at night if he wasn't allowed in the same room. He just lay around the house all day and was never allowed to go outside.

We needed to help his Earth imbalance, which was in profound, and potentially life-threatening, excess. We first started by altering his diet. First, we decreased portion size and tried to get him on a protein source, such as chicken. Ben was able to supplement the dry food with cut-up chicken breast. And we gradually weaned him off the canned food, too.

We got a little more movement of Carlton's internal *chi* by getting him to do more when Ben was around. He got Carlton a harness and leash and began walking him in the backyard. Ben also started to engage in more activities with Carlton: He responded well to hide-and-seek games that he learned to play before being fed. In this case, Ben found it difficult to change to a home-cooked meal, but we were able to make other changes that were comparatively easy: playing with Carlton more, increasing the movement of *chi* by getting the cat outdoors, and offering new stimuli in the form of toys and games that would help him to revitalize the stagnant energy in his body. In the end, we were able to change the behaviors of both pet and owner to harvest and harness some of the mutual *chi* that allowed their minds, spirits, and physical attributes to work together more harmoniously. Within six months of implementing the new regimen, Carlton had lost 3 pounds—a significant portion of his body weight—and had a lot more energy.

More Traits of Earth Pets

The Earth pet is usually the one to follow you and do whatever you ask. They typically are very poised; they want to do whatever is needed. In most cases, they are very considerate to the needs of other pets in the household.

When there is an excess of Earth, this pet can be more needy in the sense of frequently putting herself in her owner's space. This pet may get into more trouble and seem a lot less relaxed than usual, becoming increasingly anxious and quick to react to unfamiliar people and noises.

When an Earth pet is deficient, it may literally want to never let the owner out of its sight. Sometimes, when the owner leaves, the pet may become anxious and not calm down until the owner gets back.

Earth pets have a lot of difficulty with change. They do not like to get out of a routine. They may be apprehensive when faced with something new. They tend to do things the way they have always done; when faced with a new challenge, they may need some time to get comfortable with it. They are not independent pets; they need the companionship either of another owner or other pets.

The key to understanding the Earth composition is to understand that these are supportive animals. They are followers; they need to feel like they are a needed part of the whole home. They love to be involved in whatever you are doing, but they do not necessarily want to be the leader. In other words, they are great at being one of the cogs in the wheel, but they do not want to be the big wheel itself. They are looking for a secure environment, one that is premised on the owner looking out for them. At the end of the day, they just want to be loved. Earth pets seek praise from owners—as well as just about everybody else.

The problems that arise with Earth pets tend to arise out of the fact that they do not have a lot of self-confidence and will not try something new unless shown or trained. They will finish the food they are given in order to please their owner or to keep their environment in an orderly state. Not surprisingly, many Earth animals are overweight, and they have a hard time losing weight when put on a diet. Earth pets often have problems with their muscles, bones, and joints related to chronic obesity. They need to be fed on a lean basis and their weight should be measured regularly.

When an Earth pet is having problems with his digestion—meaning diarrhea, vomiting, or lack of appetite—this is usually a sign that he is out of balance and needs treatment to regain stability. If you've got an Earth pet, here are some tips for how to keep him or her in balance:

- Make a conscious effort to build your pet into your daily activities, and the activities of other members of your family. It's okay for your pet to be laid-back, but that shouldn't mean it loses out on the opportunity to interact with you or other people.

- Closely monitor your Earth pet's weight.

- You may need to take the initiative to raise the energy level a little, but once you get your Earth pet involved, you'll find that she is a lot happier and healthier.

Chapter 10

Your Metal Pet

Metal dogs are obedient and eager to carry out their next duty.

The Metal pet is tightly structured and well organized, like the element of metal itself. Metal is deeply rooted within the earth and comes into existence from years of contracting and rebuilding. It takes its core components from the earth, and builds itself up by recombining the various building blocks extracted from the earth into a solid core. Metal, though it takes varying structures, always assumes the form of a highly organized, and sometimes even sleek-looking, substance.

This is the Chinese character for Metal.

Metal requires just the right balance of raw materials to come into being. There is a clear organizing principle at the molecular level that guides both its creation and its transformation.

Metal is very particular in the relationships it fosters. Whereas Earth is grounded and engulfs everything, Metal is particular. Metal uses what it wants, when it wants to.

Characteristics of a Metal Pet

Metal-temperament pets possess similar traits to those listed above. (The accompanying table lists the characteristics, organs, and *feng shui* color associated with Metal-temperament pets.) They are deeply attached to the people they love. In fact, one distinguishing characteristic of Metal pets is the closeness of the animal's relationship to the owner; these animals tend to be extremely loyal. They also tend to be a little more skittish than other animals. If they run into a challenging situation or perceive a threat of some kind, these animals are much more likely to run and hide than they are to stand their ground. They are also remarkably keen observers of their own environment.

In the five-element system, Metal correlates to the lungs and the large intestine. Most Metal pets will have problems with these organs when they are in situations of imbalance; these problems may present themselves as coughing, wheezing, or diarrhea. The Metal pet may see flare-ups from 3:00 to 5:00 a.m. for the lungs and 5:00 to 7:00 a.m. with the large intestine. For

Element	Personality Traits	Disposition	Favorite Activities	Associated Organs	*Feng Shui Color*
Metal	Discerning, disciplined, reserved, accepting	Likes definition, structure	Performing obedience exercises, engaging in structured activities	Lungs and large intestine	Silver/ Gold

example, consider a Metal-temperament cat that is diagnosed with asthma, and then gets bouts of constipation. Some may not see a relationship between the two conditions, but in Eastern philosophies, the lungs have a way of monitoring the hydration levels or water regulation in the body. In this instance, the large intestine is compromised from the lack of water regulation, so the whole system is out of balance.

Pets with dominant Metal characteristics are usually extremely easy to identify. They may come across as more apprehensive and uncertain than other animals, and they are likely to hold their relationship with you in very high esteem indeed. Like Fire-temperament animals, they are sometimes difficult to train.

As with the other temperaments we've been examining, it's important to remember that your animal's dominant temperament may change over time.

You Probably Have a Metal-Temperament Dog If . . .

- Your dog is submissive to most or all other dogs.
- Your dog is extremely attached to you emotionally.
- Your dog seems comparatively indecisive or uncertain when you attempt to train him to do something new, or is slow to respond.

You Probably Have a Metal-Temperament Cat If . . .

- Your cat prefers to remain indoors.
- Your cat is extremely attached to you emotionally.
- Your cat spends a great deal of time grooming itself. (Metal cats may come across as self-absorbed.)
- Metal-temperament cats may also be quite thin, compared to other cats.

Twinkie

Twinkie is a petite, 11-year-old female Siamese who grooms herself constantly during the day. She cleans herself for hours: after a litter box trip, after eating, and at almost any other time. She has long fur and makes a habit of keeping herself beautiful. As far as her owner Sharon can recall, she has always had that habit. Sharon loves to brush Twinkie, and Twinkie definitely enjoys this quality time with her owner. Twinkie always wants to look immaculate and is so particular about cleanliness and grooming that Sharon has never had to give her a bath. (Many owners of purebred cats bathe their pets regularly.)

Twinkie hates going outside and will retreat to a place of safety if the front door of the home is left open for too long. She clearly prefers for the environment to remain familiar, closed, and under Sharon's control.

She knows exactly what goes on in the house and has very keen senses. She sits perched in the dining area ready to analyze any situation that arises. One day, Sharon noticed that her fur had become less glowing and that there were more mats present in her coat.

Sharon noticed that Twinkie's appetite, which was previously great, had decreased a little. Twinkie's litter box habits had become less than perfect, too, which was quite unusual for her. Sharon noticed these things, and also noted that she could hear periodic wheezing sounds when Twinkie was at rest. This, too, was unusual for this little kitty.

Cleaning the feeding area helped Twinkie regain balance in her Metal nature.

Sharon took Twinkie to a Western veterinarian, who found nothing to report. Then, sensing that something was wrong, she brought Twinkie to me.

After talking to Sharon for a while about her cat and their shared history, and after examining the living space, I examined Twinkie and then reached some conclusions. First and foremost, I determined that Twinkie had a strong Metal temperament. Second, I concluded that Twinkie was experiencing some unfortunate deficiencies in her life.

Her little body was being severely strained, mostly because of the area in which she was spending most of her time. Her feeding area had recently been moved to a dining room that was very cluttered and was often full of strange smells. To the owner's surprise, we also learned that the carpet in the dining room had mold. This environmental change had been a major strain on Twinkie's system.

The first task at hand was to give Twinkie an area that was cleaner and more conducive to a healthy flow of *chi*. We cleaned up the dining-room area and added two metal sculptures at strategically placed locations in the dining room. (We did this because I believed that the metal in her system needed support.) These simple changes had a powerful positive effect on the pet's health; a few months later, all the symptoms had receded, and her behavior was back to normal.

With Metal-temperament animals and indeed for all animals—seemingly minor changes in the pet's living environment can have a huge impact on overall health and well-being. This principle is particularly important to bear in mind when considering the predicament of Metal cats like Twinkie, who are likely to become exclusively "indoor" pets.

Unfortunately, most veterinarians will not take the time to conduct an on-site examination of the home that a pet shares with its owner. But this case study shows the importance of an in-person examination. As a result of a thorough investigation of the environment and the deficiencies Twinkie was facing, we also found out about a problem—the mold beneath the carpet—that could have been dangerous to the owner as well. Talk about a symbiotic relationship between owner and pet!

Kuma

Kuma was a 6-year-old male Akita who liked to think that he was in charge of his world.

Kuma would always sit in the living room waiting for his owners, Betsy and Hayden, to come home, so that he could go out for his scheduled walks. There was definitely a routine for Kuma. He ate breakfast at a certain time, played with his owners at a certain time, and went for walks at a certain time. Betsy and Hayden started this schedule and virtually never strayed from it.

Betsy and Hayden had been thinking for some time about getting a playmate for Kuma because he seemed to be slowing down. Often, he looked downright bored. They pondered the decision for a while, and finally decided to get a new puppy.

On the day they brought the new puppy home, Kuma did not even react to it. The puppy tried to play with Kuma, but he would have nothing to do with it.

For four weeks, Kuma simply ignored this puppy. He even started to show signs of depression. Now, when the owners came home from work, he was not there to greet them. He would eat his meals slowly and then

Kuma was shown how to be more patient and balanced.

go into another room to lie down. Betsy and Hayden thought that there was something physically wrong with him. At times, he would growl at the new puppy and even nudge it with his nose. They brought Kuma and the new puppy in to see me.

When they came into my office, it was obvious that Kuma was refusing to pay attention to the new puppy. After I reviewed their history and took a physical exam, we decided to run a blood test to make sure there was nothing wrong with Kuma. The blood test came back normal.

My diagnosis was that there seemed to be a pattern of deficiency with Kuma stemming from being a Metal dog. So, I designed some solutions to help him get his balance back. First of all, we decided that Kuma should probably sleep in Betsy and Hayden's room. I recommended this because this was a place where Kuma could feel close to his owners, secure, and in charge of his area. The puppy could not go into this area and upset him. This would help him to acclimate to the new arrival.

Second, the puppy would be put into the family room in a bordered area. This way, the new puppy would be safe and Kuma could get some peace without the little one trying to get in his bed.

Finally, Kuma would go back to his old schedule, which the new puppy had disrupted. He would be taken on his own walks and have private playtime with his owners.

After a few weeks of these changes, Kuma started to get out of his shell and even started to pay a little attention to his new friend. Before long, Kuma started to interact with the puppy more and more. Soon, the puppy and Kuma would play games of tug of war. They really started to become friends.

Why did this occur? Remember, Kuma was a Metal dog who was used to his routine and very much in tune with what his owners expected from him. When the puppy entered his life, Kuma's whole world (and schedule) changed. What's more, there was just too much chaos in the new arrangement for a highly structured dog like Kuma. Fortunately, his owners noticed the changes in behavior and took action. This is a good example of how doing things to improve your pet's temperamental balance can make a time of transition much more bearable for all parties involved.

More Traits of Metal Pets

Classic Metal pet behaviors include being very reserved and taking a step back and overlooking the environment. These pets calculate their next move. Life is almost like a chess match for them. They will observe what their owners are doing from a distance. If it is something that they are familiar with or like, then they will join in. If not, they will keep their distance but will continue to observe the happenings and outcomes.

Metal animals tend to have habits that keep their places of rest and feeding very neat. They are picky eaters because they like to analyze their food. The Metal in the pets keep them calm and subdued, but unlike Earth pets, they are subdued because they are absorbing the material around them and deciphering what is best for them to do next. They are not flamboyant with their actions and do not take uncalculated risks. They are not quick to fly off the handle. They are accepting of new surroundings and people, but will enter the new situation slowly, one step at a time.

When Metal pets have excess, they can seem confused and flustered. They may seem more standoffish, meaning that they may not be as inviting to new people or other pets as they were before. They also may show signs of becoming compulsive with their actions. For example, in a Metal cat that is out of balance due to excess, you may see the cat start to overgroom itself to the degree that it starts to tear out hair in a specific area of its body. A deficiency in the Metal pet may cause the pet to start hiding, or to give the impression of having given up on life.

Remember the following about Metal pets:

- They have tremendous difficulty dealing with disorder. They want to be the ones who are in control. They would like to rule the roost because that way, everything will go as planned.

- They do not like to be surprised by anything. They would rather be wrong than to have someone else lead them to do something.

- You should think twice before getting an animal companion for this pet. The most difficult situation for Metal pets is when a new pet is introduced into the household.

Chapter 11

Your Water Pet

Just as water flows effortlessly wherever it has to go, animals governed by this element are similarly intuitive and persistent. Water is extremely enduring. It can face many obstacles, but will always find a way to maneuver around them. Water pets present the same traits.

Water is the life-giver that constantly finds its recipient. It is the beginning of life; when it is depleted, so is the life of the creature. Without water, life would not exist.

Water can move quickly or slowly to get to its goal. It meanders and rushes in torrents; it moves through cycles; it carves new roads; it cultivates new life.

Characteristics of a Water Pet

Water animals are very smart. Given the choice, they generally prefer to sit on the periphery and oversee matters rather than mingle. Direct engagement with people and other animals does take place in their world, of course, but only on their own terms, and at a time and place of their choosing. Water animals typically prefer to find a place where they can be *near* their owner, without actually deigning to occupy the same physical space the owner is occupying. It's as though they consider their primary responsibility to be monitoring your behavior, rather than interacting with you. They save one-on-one contact for special occasions. (The table lists the characteristics, organs, and *feng shui* color associated with Water-temperament pets.)

Water pets often act like they are just part of the environment; at times, they seem hard to engage. Don't mistake this for *disengagement* though. They know exactly what is happening. And this brings us to the heart of the matter: Water animals always want to *know* what is happening around them; they just don't necessarily *approve* of everything that is taking place.

Pets with a dominant Water temperament are usually able to resolve issues that arise in their environment. They are not necessarily quick to respond to change, but are able to adjust both in mind and body to changes in their environment.

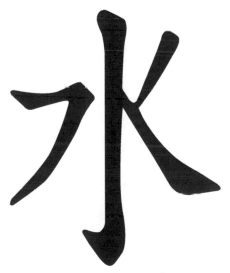

This is the Chinese character for Water.

Element	Personality Traits	Disposition	Favorite Activities	Associated Organs	*Feng Shui* Color
Water	Watchful, candid, curious, particular, self-contained and self-sufficient	Resistant to and fearful of change; prefers to be left alone	Likes to do things on his own; marches to his own drum; doesn't like organized exercise	Kidneys and urinary bladder	Blue

Water pets like to be the commanders of their domains. They love the feeling of being above everyone and everything, and are very careful in their actions. These animals usually do not like to be lap pets. They prefer to be arm's-length away, but will sometimes come closer for a little loving for a brief amount of time. Water pets usually sleep very light and are on full alert when the house is quiet.

In the five-element system, Water is associated with the urinary bladder and the kidneys. The bladder's peak activity is between 3:00 and 5:00 p.m. and the kidneys' peak activity is from 5:00 to 7:00 p.m. Water pets who are in a state of imbalance may have problems occur at these times. For example, if your Water pet gets a urinary tract infection, this may be an early sign that there is an imbalance somewhere. Kidney-related problems, such as kidney cysts or infection, can be much more serious. The kidneys are the lifeline of existence: When the kidneys wear out, so does life.

You Probably Have a Water-Temperament Dog If . . .

- Your dog somehow seems smarter than most dogs, and it's not *just* pride of ownership that makes you say that.

- Your dog prefers to sit near you, without necessarily being in your space or part of your activity, as a "default setting."

- Your dog is typically watchful and observant.

- Although pleasant enough, your dog is unlikely to have extreme, highly energetic displays of affection with people. "Dignified" or "reserved" are common adjectives used to describe these dogs.

You Probably Have a Water-Temperament Cat If . . .

- Your cat seems smarter than most cats, and it's not *just* pride of ownership that makes you say that.

- Your cat is not quick to interact with human beings, and frequently perches on the highest, most easily accessible surface to watch the proceedings in your home.

- Your cat appears to enjoy overseeing things, and watches the world pass by in much the same way a head of state would.

Honeypie

Honeypie was a 13-year-old domestic shorthaired cat of mixed, but nevertheless superior, breed. She spent years perfecting the air of a wise sage with detached authority, which endeared her to her owner, Mike. She had never been an extremely sociable cat. Lately, however, Mike sensed that she had become even more withdrawn than usual. Instead of greeting Mike and other people in the house briefly once or twice a day, with tail held high in the air (as had been her habit for some time), now she had almost completely abandoned the practice of holding court with human beings. She seemed so sedentary and withdrawn, in fact, that Mike began to worry about her. He asked me to examine her.

When I did, I found that the layout of Honeypie's main living and sleeping area seemed likely to both disrupt her sleep and deplete her *chi* flow. After talking to Mike, I concluded that this had been the case for some time. Honeypie's prime "court" was now out in the family dining

Honeypie's surroundings are her palace.

area. She once strode about this area proudly inspecting her domain; nowadays, though, she seemed content to find a secluded corner of the room in which to hide. As far as I could tell, she was avoiding people and keeping almost entirely to herself. Mike confirmed as much. When I conducted a full physical examination, I found more bad news: Honeypie's kidneys were not functioning well.

I talked with Mike about all of this and together we planned some changes meant not only to help improve Honeypie's kidney function, but also to help her become more sociable. We made some dietary changes, but perhaps the most important changes were those we made to the physical environment, which I sensed had been steadily degrading Honeypie's *chi* flow. I suggested to Mike that he set up a cat tree in an unused guest bedroom in a spot that would promote good *chi* . . . and that would also give Honeypie a commanding, high-level view of the proceedings in the family dining room that had previously been her base of operations.

Honeypie's diet and living environment were now in balance. Her new living space, complete with a new cat bed and that attractive new perching area, became her throne room. It was an appealing, secluded spot where Honeypie could *either* monitor what was going on in the house *or* descend to her chambers and get the uninterrupted rest she needed. The choice was hers.

The main lesson to draw from this case is that there are a multitude of things that can go astray with any pet. Each and every pet who falls out of balance deserves the chance to come back into balance in order to achieve harmony.

Honeypie responded quickly and positively to these changes. Within a few weeks, her kidney function improved and she was once again inspecting the peasants—excuse me, human beings—who occupied her domain on a regular basis. When guests came into Mike's house, they were again subjected, when schedules permitted, to an inspection from Honeypie—the reigning monarch.

Jeremy

Pictured here is a Border Collie cross; Border Collies are known for intelligence.

Jeremy was a 9-year-old Border Collie mix. Jeremy loved to be with his owner, Jack, and was his constant companion. The dog would always take a back seat to whatever activity was going on in the home.

Jack, a film producer, lived a very stressful life. He had erratic hours and sometimes would not feed Jeremy until late at night—but Jack would never forget Jeremy's two walks per day.

Jeremy would eat well one day and the next day he would barely eat at all, but he loved being taken on walks where he could use his intelligence to help navigate Jack's path. The erratic eating habits went on for months at a time and eventually brought on bouts of diarrhea and vomiting. This is when Jack brought Jeremy in to see me.

We did an in depth Q-and-A session and I was able to determine that Jeremy was indeed a Water dog. He was very intelligent, and he loved to sit on the back of the sofa and oversee everything that was going on in his living space. He would sleep on Jack's bed—but not too close.

I also learned that Jeremy's sleeping habits were erratic. We took a blood test and some X-rays. The blood test showed a mild elevation in his pancreas but otherwise was unremarkable. The X-rays did not show anything, so we opted to do an ultrasound. The ultrasound showed stomach ulcers and some small-intestinal ulcers.

Jeremy was stressing out—and now Jack was even more stressed out than usual. The dog he loved was in pain. We set up a plan of action. First of all, we gradually introduced a new diet for Jeremy; it consisted of turkey, brown rice, squash, and some *tripe* (the stomach lining of cows or sheep). The tripe deserves some explanation: In Eastern philosophies, many experts believe that supporting the problematic organ with food that is made of the same organ can help replenish some of the lost vitality.

Jeremy took to this diet very well; Jack told me that he had not seen Jeremy eat like this since he was a puppy.

At that point, I told Jack that he needed to calm his own schedule and establish a predictable feeding routine for Jeremy. The stress was affecting Jeremy to the extent that the *chi* imbalance was now manifesting with stomach ulcers. Jack's chaotic hours were throwing off Jeremy's balance—and his own. Jack agreed to make his days more predictable, thereby providing a routine for Jeremy.

The other treatment that we implemented was to give Jeremy acupuncture therapy to open channels (meridians) and to assist the flow of *chi* throughout the body. I felt this would help to restore balance and would also support the healing of the stomach.

After six months, Jack brought Jeremy into the office for a routine checkup. Jeremy looked much better; his stomach problems were much less pronounced and the ulcers had begun to heal. He seemed much more relaxed and Jack also looked good and rested.

More Traits of Water Pets

Water pets that are in excess may not be as sharp as usual. For instance, these animals may no longer opt for a high vantage point. They may seek more attention from their owners; sometimes owners find them sitting on their laps more. Because of this, owners typically feel that their pet has become more "sociable." In reality, the animal is seeking some type of shelter from the owner.

Deficient Water pets can be very moody. For example, they may want to be petted sometimes but not at other times. They may be spooked very easily by noises or new people. Their sleep patterns can be very erratic and easily interrupted, and their eating habits can change rapidly. These pets can eat very well one day and not so well the next. At times they can look miserable and lost.

Water pets often have problems with new pets or people. They do not seem to trust people from the onset. They do not always have the confidence to be bold and interrelational. They may have trouble when they have to move out of their own comfort zone by sharing their space with other pets. They can learn to be with other animals, but need to be introduced to them slowly.

Here are some tips for managing your Water pet:

- Water pets want a safe, accessible place from which to survey all the activity in the home. Provide it!

- Water pets often seem to understand exactly what you are talking about, but as smart as they are, they do not like to be the center of attention. Following commands and performing tricks may not be their forte.

- Both Water cats and Water dogs will relish the opportunity to observe from a distance. They may prefer access to a high vantage point in the environment.

- Water cats, in particular, need cat trees or other easily accessible perches that allow them to review everything that is taking place in their domain. (This is true of many cats, but Water cats need this perch more than others because of their reclusiveness.) And remember—the home is their domain, not yours. You are merely lucky enough to serve as caretaker for a property that is occupied by a more intelligent and refined being.

Chapter 12

Your Wood Pet

The final temperament to look at is the Wood temperament. Again, please remember that each of the elemental temperaments I've discussed here may well show up in combination with another temperament.

This Wood cat, with ears drawn back, is displaying a classic fight-or-flight response.

An animal may present more than one element, but will usually have one that dominates; a given animal's temperament may change over time, too.

Wood is very bold; it starts from a conglomeration of particles and is able to present itself at any point. Wood is unpredictable because no one knows when it will start its cycle. One day there may be nothing and the next there is change and a budding of new hope.

Wood gathers all its resources and then uses those resources to proliferate in a way that can be as massive as a forest. The nourishment of Wood comes from many sources. Wood tackles something it has not known before and uses its boldness to conquer it. Wood grows steadily and con-fidently; it may encounter obstacles, but it continues on its journey to attain its goal.

This is the Chinese character for Wood.

Characteristics of a Wood Pet

The bottom line on animals with a dominant Wood temperament is that they're bold, deeply wary of outsiders, and sometimes a little skit-tish. They are known to overreact when they misread someone's inten-tions. They may have very warm, close relationships with people and other animals . . . but outsiders are likely to find them aloof or downright hostile. In extreme cases, they may move quickly into fight-or-flight mode, and adopt fearful or aggressive attitudes to anyone they feel has intruded on their space or compromised their sense of personal safety. (The table lists the characteristics, organs, and *feng shui* color associated with Wood-temperament pets.)

A Wood pet typically has a bold nature and tries to oversee its ter-ritory with a presence of boldness. These pets may even shift their ears back or make the hair on the back of the neck stand up to signal to an opponent that an attack will result if the threatener does not back away. They have amazing confidence when it comes to protecting what is important to them. They are quick to lash out: They come from the school of "attack first, ask questions later." These animals usually have one speed: On.

Element	Personality Traits	Disposition	Favorite Activities	Associated Organs	Feng Shui Color
Wood	Confident, assertive, bold, competitive, powerful	Very aggressive; loves action, movement, and adventure; likes to be first	Aggressive play with pull toys; uses her mouth to play games	Liver and gallbladder	Green

Wood animals inspire a certain amount of awe, and they know it. This is their personality and they are willing to battle for it. Some people try to break Wood animals of their habits, but this is their inner vitality and people should learn to adapt to their pets' behavior. To break down this deep inner structure would be detrimental for the pet in the future.

The Wood pet in excess may show strong signs of aggression when faced with new people and new surroundings. This may not always be pleasant, but it needs to be taken care of before more drastic incidents occur. These pets are sometimes described as "enraged" or "uncontrollable," but it is usually more accurate to say that they are fully engaged in situations where they are threatened. Some people say that this can be a state of rage. They may also experience skin problems and muscle problems manifesting from back or leg injuries.

The deficient Wood pet may show signs of fatigue. This pet may also have problems with excessive scratching, accompanied by skin problems. Ear infections can also manifest. A Wood pet's body may show signs of weakness, as well as back problems and weakness in the hindquarters. It is not uncommon for deficient Wood pets to experience chronic illness.

You Probably Have a Wood-Temperament Dog If . . .

• Your dog acts erratically when around others.

• Your dog has been known to "act out" by nipping or biting.

- Your dog is described as "high-strung" or "easily upset."
- Your dog is close and friendly with you, but deeply wary of other people.
- People think your dog overreacts to other humans or animals, or has trouble socializing.
- *You* think your dog overreacts to other humans or animals, or has trouble socializing.

You Probably Have a Wood-Temperament Cat If . . .

- Your cat is all about boundaries: "Don't bother me. Keep your distance."
- Your cat rarely or never interacts with strangers.
- Your cat hisses or finds other ways to "act out" with people who try to make contact.
- People think your cat overreacts to other humans or animals, or has trouble socializing.
- *You* think your cat overreacts to other humans or animals, or has trouble socializing.

Fancy

Fancy, a 10-year-old female Collie mix, developed severe hot spots with nonstop itching, scratching, and biting. She was always high-strung and startled easily, according to her owners, but now she seemed focused only on her skin problem. Her owners tried all the topical lotions and creams that were supposed to fix the skin problems—both over-the-counter varieties and prescribed medications. Nothing worked.

Her owners came to me for help. After spending some time discussing Fancy's condition, I suggested that we change the dog's diet to correct what appeared to be a Wood excess in her system. To compensate, we changed Fancy's diet to incorporate rice, tuna, and olive oil.

In a matter of days, the itching and scratching was reduced. Within a few weeks, the improvement was even more apparent and Fancy was back to the normal, if slightly edgy, behavior pattern that her owners had come to expect from her.

Dante

Dante was a 2-year-old male rescue dog, a mix of Terrier, Poodle, and Whippet. He was very boisterous and quick to act out at anyone he did not know. He had a very intense fight-or-flight response and was quick to fight.

On the outside, Dante came across as being "crazy," but I could tell that in actuality he wasn't "crazy" at all; he was just very decisive in both his likes and his dislikes. After talking to his owners, I was able to determine that he was fed regularly twice per day; I also learned that he got restless at night and often woke his owners to let him out. He had recently become a little more aggressive; when his owners took him to visit the groomer, he would get particularly anxious when the groomer tried to bathe him.

Dante was boisterous and quick to act up.

Dante's normal hangout spot in the house was the bedroom. Because he was showing excess in his Wood constitution, I felt we needed to find something that would balance him. We decided to close off the bedroom and put him into a new area in the family room that would use the Fire element to balance out the Wood element more effectively than the bedroom had. We placed a red bed in the family room and also put in lamps with red shades—both Fire sources that could help him burn off some of that excess Wood. The food choice that we made was to add some lamb to his diet, which would also burn off the Wood.

Dante responded very well and after harmonizing him we were able to decrease some of the Wood so he didn't have any problems with excess in his system. It's always important to keep a balance because your pet's system—like your own—is always changing.

Dante no longer seemed "crazy." The changes we made helped him to adapt more effectively to his environment and the people in it . . . and to win him and his owners a little more time before Dante shifted into fight-or-flight mode.

More Traits of Wood Pets

Wood pets can become very frustrated when they realize they are not capable of doing something they were once able to do. This is a common problem because they work and play intensely and push their bodies to the limits. In fact, these animals are comparable to a human professional athlete. They compete hard, and often pay for it the next day. They have great difficulty being inactive and need constant exercise and praise. These pets love to play and be played with, and they love focused games. Wood pets enjoy hide-and-seek and they display a need for constant stimulation. They are highly competitive and extremely strong-willed.

In particular, the Wood pet in excess needs help in finding balance and calming the intensity in order to create harmony in mind, body, and spirit.

Wood dogs are often perceived as being very erratic in behavior—kind of like a person who's had too many cups of coffee. Wood cats bring a slightly different spin to the temperament: They may seem a bit like a reclusive billionaire, someone who simply doesn't want to connect with "undesirables," who doesn't feel he or she has to connect, who can afford not to connect, and is willing to go to great lengths to avoid ever having to connect. If you're foolish enough to try to get past a Wood animal's security measures . . . well, let's just say that you may find the results unpleasant.

Wood is associated with the liver and gallbladder. With imbalances, you may see problems with these organs. For example, in the case of a dog that is exposed to a toxin, the liver will try to overcome the burden it is faced with by filtering and trying to remove the inciting toxin. The time of day that the liver may show its peak is between 1:00 and 3:00 a.m. The gallbladder will likely show its peak between 11:00 p.m. and 1:00 a.m.

Here are some tips for understanding a Wood pet:

- A Wood pet wants barriers, familiarity, and a sense of control over the environment. Provide it!

- Help people who don't know your pet to learn what kind of distance your pet expects from strangers, and how long it usually takes for your pet to get to know someone.

- Be ready to address excessive Wood behavior with simple changes in the environment that can rectify the behavior, such as the addition of red lights or coverings in the animal's sleeping area.

Chapter 13

Managing Common Life Transitions

When your life changes dramatically, your pet's life changes dramatically, too. The quality of your relationship with your pet depends in large measure on the way you as a pet owner manage those shared transitions.

Your pet gives you a great deal of joy; she always seems to be there when you need a pick-me-up. When big transitions happen in your life, as they will, you owe your pet something in return. You owe her a little foresight and a little accommodation. You owe your pet some one-on-one time. And you owe her some help with the recognition that when your life changes in major ways, she, too, will be managing transitions, and she, too, may need some help.

Animals are more sensitive to change than most pet owners realize, and some life transformations present particularly difficult challenges for both pets and owners. This chapter offers some case studies incorporating some of the most important life-change scenarios; identifies some of the challenges inherent in each scenario; and shows how to respond in a balanced, supportive way that respects both the inevitability of change and the principles of *feng shui*.

> *To everything there is a season, and a time to every purpose under heaven.*
>
> —*Ecclesiastes*

Just like a chick emerging from a shell, you and your
pet are always navigating transitions.

Polly

Polly was a 10-year-old Labrador Retriever who was deeply in love with
Deirdre, her owner. *Love* really is the appropriate word here. Polly had
been with Deirdre since she was a puppy, and the two had built an
exceptionally strong bond over the years.

As you might expect, Polly was used to being the center of attention
when Deirdre was around. She had spent her entire life as Deirdre's closest friend and ally. The two did just about everything together: go for
walks and jogs, take vacations, you name it. For the past five years,
Deirdre had been lucky enough to be able to work from home . . . which
meant that she spent most of her waking hours in Polly's company,
which Polly enjoyed a great deal.

Then the change came.

Polly and her owner eventually found harmony in their new life.

Deirdre hadn't dated seriously since Polly was about 2 years old, but she met a friend named Matt online—a friend who shared so many of her interests that she decided to start seeing him. Matt seemed perfect: He was about Deirdre's age; he was caring, considerate, and attentive; and he took a special interest in Deirdre's profession (technical writing). He'd even grown up with dogs and loved them—though he didn't have one of his own right then.

Deirdre started spending more and more time with Matt, which meant leaving Polly on her own in the apartment for long stretches of time. That had happened only intermittently in the past, but it became the norm. Two or three nights a week, Polly was alone in the apartment while Deirdre spent time with Matt. Sometimes, Deirdre even brought her laptop to Matt's apartment so she could get work done there during the day. She checked in on Polly regularly, of course—but not regularly enough to suit Polly's tastes.

About two weeks after she began spending a great deal of time with Matt, Deirdre noticed some strange changes in Polly's behavior. Despite regular walks—"twice a day, just like always," Deirdre told me—Polly began doing her business inside the apartment. "It was like she completely forgot that she was housetrained," Deirdre said. "It was just bizarre." In addition, the dog seemed skittish and anxious, which were not behaviors that Deirdre was used to seeing in Polly. As if all of that weren't enough, Polly developed some serious digestive problems.

A conventional Western approach to Polly's condition might have focused exclusively on the dog's digestive issues. A Western-medicine veterinarian might not even have taken the time to ask questions about the major changes that had recently taken place in the dog's world. When Deirdre came to me for help, however, I asked not only about Polly's behavior and physical symptoms, but also about the history and current state of her relationship with Deirdre. It was at that point that I learned how close the two had been over the last decade—and how very different Polly's life was right now. For instance, the walks that were happening twice a day, "just like always," were now lasting five or ten minutes instead of twenty to thirty.

I told Deirdre that Polly seemed to be in the middle of what human beings would call a life crisis. From her point of view, the closest relationship in her life, the only relationship that mattered to her—her relationship to Deirdre, her "alpha dog"—lay in ruins. She had been accustomed to receiving virtually all of Deirdre's attention, and now Deirdre had abandoned her, materializing only sporadically to refill Polly's food bowl and take her for all-too-brief walks. Polly was experiencing physical symptoms, yes, but she was also "acting out"—and was having a difficult time calming down, even while Deirdre was spending time with her. The episodes of her fouling the apartment were best understood as protests from someone who was deeply unhappy with the direction a relationship with a loved one had taken.

I made it clear to Deirdre that a big part of the solution was going to involve her relationship with Polly. If she continued the pattern of paying virtually no attention to Polly and simply left it to me to "fix" the physical symptoms, we weren't going to get anywhere. On the other hand, if she and I approached the problem together, in an integrated way, and found a way to give Polly more of the attention and respect she had come to expect and felt that she deserved, we would probably be able to make some headway.

Fortunately, we did make headway. By changing her protein source to lamb, we were able to tone down some of her problems with excesses in her Wood constitution. We moved Polly's sleeping area to a different spot in the house that I felt would help relax her. Just as important, Deirdre made some major changes in the way she interacted with her dog. She made it a point to have more positive interactions with Polly and to spend at least half an hour a day with her, one-on-one.

After a little less than two weeks of receiving more focused attention from Deirdre, taking advantage of some nutritional changes, and enjoying a new sleeping space, Polly's toilet habits returned to normal. Owner and dog were in balance again . . . because they had begun the process of navigating the changes in life together.

This example shows how changing just a few things in a pet's world can deliver great rewards for both pet and owner.

Just as with your human loved ones, your pet benefits from the quality of the attention you share with her. That attention has a major impact on your pet's well-being and sense of self—and, I believe, on the flow of *chi* that you both experience. You must always remember that there is a highly interactive form of energy exchanged among you, your pet, and the other people around you. This energy can either flow very comfortably around and within you, or it can be choked off and disturbed. The changes you must manage in your life will always be easier to navigate if you take actions that support the energy's free flow, like a scarf that moves smoothly through the wind. Of course, there will be times when *chi* is blocked or deflected. When this happens, you as a pet owner need to be responsive to the situation in order to help your pet get through these times of uneasiness, and look for ways to restore her—and your—connection to the effortless, life-giving energy flow.

A little of this energy can go a very long way, as Polly and Deirdre's case shows. It turned out that Polly didn't need *all* of Deirdre's time and attention in order to function well and make the transition—she just needed enough attention to be reassured that she was still part of the "pack."

I don't think Deirdre realized the effect that suddenly withdrawing her attention from Polly would have on both of their lives. When she started spending all of her available time with Matt, she saw herself as moving on in her life. What she didn't realize, at least at first, was that Polly needed some help moving on as well.

All too often, pet owners simply turn the page in their own lives without stopping to think about the impact their decisions will have on the pets whom they love and who love them.

Mickey and Minnie

Mickey and Minnie were happy members of the Barclay family. This brother and sister were calm, observant, domestic shorthaired cats who spent most of their time in an unused bedroom on the upper floor of the Barclay home.

Then the change happened: Mrs. Barclay became pregnant. About seven months into her term, Mr. Barclay got serious about setting up the nursery. That nursery was to occupy the bedroom where Mickey and Minnie spent most of their time. Without much thought or fanfare, the frisky pair were relegated to the home's large basement.

At first, the move wasn't much of a problem for the cats. There were a lot of empty boxes in the basement, which meant a lot of new spaces in which to play. The cats almost seemed to prefer the new space, and didn't seem to mind that their food, toys, and litter boxes had been moved to various corners of the basement. But then the big day came: Mrs. Barclay gave birth to twins.

Mickey and Minnie did not relish the addition of new family members, but learned to integrate the new babies into their lives.

The two new arrivals really threw Mickey and Minnie for a loop. All of the attention was going to these two new, strange creatures! Mickey and Minnie suddenly became quite anxious and started acting out. It was as though they had realized why they had been exiled from their own room, and realized that they didn't like it one bit. Suddenly, the two cats were incapable of interacting harmoniously with their owners, and their reactions around the babies were so hostile that the new parents were genuinely concerned for their children's safety.

This was a real challenge because the parents were understandably busy attending to the new members of their family. They weren't getting a lot of sleep, and they didn't have time, energy, or desire to deal with this problem with the cats. With their home life in chaos, they came to me for help.

Of course, no one could blame them for being distracted during the period leading up to the birth of their babies . . . but the fact remained that the Barclays had not yet given their cats a real chance to integrate themselves into the new household. As a result of what seemed to Mickey and Minnie to be a sudden and completely unexpected change in family dynamics, they had gone from being thoughtful, observant cats to being anxious, aggressive, and resentful outsiders.

The first order of business was to find a peaceful new area for the cats, a place where they could interact with the owners and, at the same time, safely observe the new babies from time to time and establish for themselves that the newcomers did not constitute a threat. The cats had to be able to integrate into the situation at their own pace. I found the calmest area of the house and set up a space for them there. I also made some changes in their diet to compensate for the excess Water and excess Wood behaviors Minnie and Mickey were exhibiting: detachment and aggressiveness, respectively.

We found that the cats responded well. They simply needed to be able to process the big changes in their surroundings in a way that made sense for them. To help make sure that happened, we gave them a place where it was easy for them to calm down and start to feel like part of the family again; we also gave them time to adjust on their own terms.

Harmony quickly returned to the home.

Just like human beings, pets often don't like surprises, and they certainly don't like feeling as though the people they love have been cutting them out of the action. That's what the basement environment ended up feeling like for Mickey and Minnie. With a little bit of help from me, the Barclays created a new, more-inclusive environment that helped the cats to calm down; to rediscover their observant, placid side; and to make the transition to the new experience that was going on in the household.

For nothing is fixed, forever and forever and forever, it is not fixed; the earth is always shifting, the light is always changing, the sea does not cease to grind down rock. Generations do not cease to be born, and we are responsible to them because we are the only witnesses they have. The sea rises, the light fails, lovers cling to each other, and children cling to us. The moment we cease to hold each other, the sea engulfs us and the light goes out.

—James Baldwin, American novelist

Selma and the New Puppy

Trouble on the home front was the last thing anyone expected from Selma.

Selma was a 15-year-old, female Jack Russell Terrier. She had been living in the same house for twelve years, and one got the feeling that she considered Jack and Mike, the two young boys who lived with her, to be her own puppies. Her owners, Mal and Celia, had encouraged a close and loving relationship between the kids and the beautiful, matronly dog for years. Trouble on the home front from Selma was the last thing anyone would have expected. Then came the change.

One day Mal and Celia agreed, after months of pleading, to let Jack and Mike pick out a brand-new puppy at the pet store. When they brought Simon home—a mixed-breed, Wood-temperament dog—the dynamic in the house changed dramatically.

Selma, an Earth dog, had gotten used to being the "ruler" of the house. She was always the special one, the one the boys paid attention to, and she was the one who controlled and secured the territory. When the boys brought the new puppy home, her life was thrown into turmoil. So, from time to time, was the household. Selma had no patience for the upstart new arrival and she was often aggressive toward Simon. She was also, the family learned, quite loud when she wanted to be.

Pet owners sometimes don't take into account the fact that animals, like humans, have less tolerance for change as they age. Mal and Celia realized this only after the fact, but they still didn't want to deprive their boys of the new puppy with whom the whole family had fallen in love. They called me for advice.

This household needed a lot of careful balancing in order to return it to a state of harmony. Here was an energetic young animal, new on the scene, and an older dog who had lost some of her vitality, but who was still accustomed to assuming the lead position. Rather than deny the queen her sense of domain, the owners and I decided to separate the two animals and to let the energetic young Simon frolic with the boys in a separate space. I also suggested that we change Selma's sleeping area to a spot in the house where the flow of *chi* would be more likely to leave her feeling revived—and in full authority over her surroundings—upon awakening.

I'm happy to report that the house is now in a state of balance.

Change is certain. Peace is followed by disturbances; departure of evil men by their return. Such recurrences should not constitute occasions for sadness but realities for awareness, so that one may be happy in the interim.

—The I Ching *(ancient Chinese classical text)*

Animals Face Big Transitions of Their Own

So far, I've been sharing stories of how human beings made (or inherited) big changes in their lives that affected the lives of their pets. There have also been plenty of cases in my practice where the major life transitions were ones experienced first and foremost by *pets*, and the owners found a way to adjust to the new situation together—as partners.

There are too many such cases for me to list here, but one particularly moving case is so hard for me to forget that it seems worth mentioning. A 10-year-old male Dalmatian, who had been adopted by his owners just six months earlier, developed a cancerous growth on the leg.

The only option the owners felt comfortable with was an amputation of the leg. They felt that by amputating they could take their dog out of a state of perpetual pain. Other options, such as chemotherapy, did not seem right for them or for their pet. (Putting the dog down was not an option the owners wanted to consider.)

After the dog healed from the surgery, the owners sought me out for help in balancing his system, toning his muscles, and helping him adjust to life using three legs. As a practitioner, I knew we had another goal, as well: to support his system to keep the cancer from resurfacing. I did this by starting an acupuncture regimen on the pet. He responded well to this and so far has not had any recurrence of cancer.

I will always remember how much work the owners did to adjust their living environment to the needs of this recently adopted pet. They made him a ramp that made it easier for him to go in and out of the house, and they set up carpeting (runners) on the hardwood floors to make it easier for him to get around.

Just as important, the owners gave the dog plenty of time to adjust and didn't pressure him in any way. The dog slowly adjusted to the situation and has kept up a remarkably high quality of life—quite an accomplishment, considering how many veterinarians, and pet owners, would have "addressed" this major life change by simply ending the animal's life when the disease presented itself. I wonder how many human cancer patients would accept that approach.

Change Happens

There are a whole host of changes and life transitions that your pet may need some help adapting to. Here are a few examples.

The first example is the change that takes place when you move from one home to another. A cat who grew up in a home where the neighborhood was its environment has a tremendous stress going on in its body when it is moved into a whole new environment, even one that is comparable to the old environment. Problems that may occur include catfights, staying out for longer periods, meowing constantly, and looking to get out of the house. You may take it for granted that your pet will adjust to a move as easily as you do, but often this is not the case. The underlying reason for a pet's inability to adjust is that it was never able to process the fact that it was going to be faced with a change in the environment. No, you can't communicate verbally with a pet about such things, but you can do things that make such life changes more bearable. One good idea is to take your pet to the new home for short periods of time before you move in to get it used to the new place. This can help ease the stress of change in your pet's life—and yours.

Another change area where a pet can easily become stressed comes from the introduction of a new person or animal to the environment. This could be a new baby, a life companion, or another pet. Here again, gradualism and respect for the animal's role in the household should be the guiding principles. For example, a new baby is brought into the home. Before the baby even arrives, try introducing your pet to the baby's room for extended periods. Play lullabies so the pet has a chance to get used to the changed environment. You may even think about having a recording of a baby crying and play this at different lengths of time. Once the baby arrives, bring home a blanket from the hospital that has the baby's smell on it; let your pet smell the blanket and possibly even roll in it or sleep on it. Becoming familiar with the scent before the baby actually arrives can help your pet to process the drastic change that the new addition to the household represents.

Finally, there are situations where your pet is deprived of contact with you, which can be downright traumatic for the pet. Your pet may react to these sudden and unexpected changes—such as a stay in a boarding facility—in a variety of different ways. Depending on the animal's temperament, you may see responses that range from vomiting or diarrhea to changed eating and sleeping patterns, or even increased agitation and aggression. All involve sudden changes in temperament and demeanor, and all can be connected to the owner's sudden disappearance from the animal's life.

These symptoms are all signals that you, the owner, have failed the "gradualism" test, and now need to find a way to spend a little more one-on-one time with your pet in a welcoming, loving environment. (For all your pet knows, after all, you have vanished altogether.)

If you're planning to put your pet in a kennel, you should make a couple of visits to the facility together in order to allow the animal to develop some familiarity with the place. If at all possible, you should also find a way to visit with your pet during its stay. Beyond this, it is unwise to make generalizations. If you notice any of the symptoms I've listed above, don't wait until your pet is reunited with you. Consult one of the veterinarians listed in the Appendix and arrange for an examination, so you can get a better sense of what your pet's symptoms mean, and what changes—beyond simply spending more time with your pet—you can make to improve the situation, even in your absence.

Such attentiveness to the relationship is important to your pet's health and well-being. There are physical problems that can present or accelerate differently in response to change, depending on the temperament of the animal. For instance, in response to the stress associated with a major change in environment, a Water dog may be more likely to have kidney or bone problems.

The Journey Together

What should you learn from all this? One lesson is that a qualified practitioner can make a huge difference in your pet's ability to adjust to new surroundings and incorporate new situations. Perhaps just as important, though, is the lesson that change is inevitable. How you respond to change defines you. We all face changes as we journey through life, and we all have company as we encounter those changes. For those who are lucky enough to be pet owners, animals are among the beloved fellow travelers on that trip. They are part of the journey. Your relationship with your pet should matter enough for you to treat her with the care, foresight, and respect she has earned while traveling with you.

Of course, everyone must navigate change in life, and you cannot always accommodate all the preferences of the animal you love. Nor can you anticipate or prepare for every physical change that is likely to affect your pet. You can, however, recognize the need of your pet to navigate such life changes *with you*. You can also be sensitive to your pet's need for continuity and familiarity. And you can respect her need for focused energy and attention from you as you make the inevitable, and often difficult, transitions that are part of human (and animal) existence.

Today, it's perhaps a little too easy to forget that a pet is not simply an accessory in your life, to be changed like curtains or cell phones when fashions shift or new priorities emerge. Pets are true companions who help to make the journey worthwhile. When you decide to "turn a corner," as you inevitably will, take a moment to think of all that your pet does to make the journey you have undertaken rich and rewarding. Bearing that in mind, you should find a way to bring your pet along to your next destination in a way that shows how much you have valued, and continue to value, her company along the way. Neither humans nor animals can avoid change—you can only adjust to change in a way that honors what has gone before and celebrates what has remained with you.

Without accepting the fact that everything changes, we cannot find perfect composure. But unfortunately, although it is true, it is difficult for us to accept it. Because we cannot accept the truth of transience, we suffer.

—*Shunryu Suzuki, Buddhist priest*

Chapter 14

Frequently Asked Questions

Having a Q-and-A session with your vet is essential when determining your pet's overall wellness.

Like every veterinarian, I hear questions from pet owners that come up over and over again. In this chapter, I share some of the most common questions I hear, as well as my responses, which are based on the best interests of the pet and take into account both Eastern and Western veterinary perspectives. My hope is that what follows will help you to make intelligent choices in your own situation.

How much exercise does my pet need?

Pets and people need a good exercise program to help keep them mentally, physically, and spiritually healthy.

The exact amount of physical exercise your pet needs each day depends on the breed of the animal, the physical nature of the pet, how the pet has been eating, and other factors. There are basically two kinds of exercise for pets: physical exercise and mental exercise. These forms of exercise work best when they're interconnected, which is another way of saying that you should be on the lookout for activities that not only stimulate your pet's body, but also stimulate your pet's mind.

A good rule of thumb is that dogs need two daily walks of about half an hour each. Even if you have to cut the walk short, your dog should get out twice a day! Make sure the walks allow your dog to move along at a brisk pace. Mental exercise for dogs typically means playing games with them such as throwing a ball or hiding bones, training them to perform some behavior, setting up an obstacle course, taking them for a ride in the car, or walking them near busy areas.

As a general rule, cats need two daily sessions of physical playtime. This might include running around, swatting at a fly that was unfortunate enough to make it into your house, or engaging in some other kind of vigorous activity. Some cats do this kind of activity on their own, but others need a little encouragement. For cats in the latter category, good opportunities for mental stimulation could range from playing with cat toys to spontaneous games you create around acquiring food or treats. Just about anything you do to get your cat's attention, including makeshift obstacle courses you set up in the home for them, counts as mental stimulation. Cat trees—climbing structures covered with carpeting—are another good addition to the environment that will promote physical and mental exercise.

With pets such as rodents and reptiles, you can provide both kinds of stimulation by using different mazes and toys. Change the environment regularly! This helps with mental exercise.

You must remind yourself constantly that total wellness does not pertain solely to the exercise of the body. The Western world sometimes perceives wellness as keeping in shape to maintain a low-fat body and having a good-looking body. These considerations are only part of the equation. The Eastern world knows that the other part of wellness comes from balancing the channels within the body and the mind. It's important to keep channels open and to promote healthy *chi* flow, and to understand that the goal of physical exercise—and many other activities—is to balance body and mind.

I talked to my veterinarian, and he said he couldn't be responsible for my pet's health if I adopted a course of treatment that included acupuncture. What should I do?

Veterinary acupuncture has been used for a long time and has been proven to work very effectively. Pets are the best acupuncture patients. There is no placebo effect with them; animals do not pretend or believe that they feel better when they truly don't.

Despite the skepticism of those who are unfamiliar with it, acupuncture is an effective alternative treatment for both pets and humans. It has been used with success for thousands of years. When administered by a qualified practitioner, there are both long-term and short-term benefits, and no side effects. This mode of treatment has a great track record.

Do some research on the subject and share your findings with your vet. The more information you share, the more likely your vet will have a better reaction. A good place to start learning more about alternative approaches to veterinary medicine is the American Holistic Veterinary Medical Association. Its Website is www.ahvma.org. Another good site to check out is the American Academy of Veterinary Acupuncture, which may be found at www.aava.org.

If all else fails, see the Appendix for a list of veterinarians who can incorporate alternative treatment for your pet.

How does acupuncture work? Why does it get the results that it does?

An acupuncture treatment.

I believe there is an energy that creates and sustains our larger world, and I believe the body works the same way. A body can become ill from energy stoppages like environmental toxins, blocked *chi* flow, and the like. Acupuncture has various methods, including dry needling, aquapuncture, and electroacupuncture. By using one of these methods, an acupuncturist stimulates the areas of the body that keep energy flowing, which helps to maintain harmony in the system. Acupuncture establishes pathways for energy and compensates for energy blockages, or opens them up, so that the body can run efficiently and effectively.

How does this happen, exactly? Here's a short explanation: The body has multiple meridians (pathways); points located along each meridian are associated with various organ systems. These points, which are in both pets and humans, are then manipulated through acupuncture techniques for a particular medical ailment in order to keep energy flowing.

What can I do if I can't afford acupuncture?

There are some low-cost alternatives to acupuncture that also open up energy channels, but they involve the use of Chinese herbs that are classified as prescription drugs. Find an experienced, knowledgeable, and trusted veterinarian in your area who is familiar with alternative practices, and with whom you can discuss Chinese herbal options for your pet. You'll find a list of alternative veterinary practitioners in the Appendix. You may also want to take a look at the *Clinical Handbook of Chinese Veterinary Herbal Medicine*, by Signe Beebe, DVM, Michael Salewski, DVM, Lorena Monda, DOM, and John Scott, DOM. It's available through Golden Flower Chinese Herbs, at www.gfcherbs.com/catalog.

Will acupuncture needles hurt my pet?

There are no known adverse effects in pets from the insertion of needles during acupuncture treatments.

Absolutely not. Unfortunately, many pet owners have developed a fear of needles, which may expand into phobias that affect their treatment choices for their pets. You feel a slight sensation at the puncture site when undergoing acupuncture treatment, but no pain. To reassure pet owners, I often put a needle in my own hand to demonstrate that there is no pain. A good practitioner will establish a rapport with your pet, and allow your pet to relax enough so there are no problems. Human patients may need more help than animals when it comes to relaxing before an acupuncture treatment.

How can *feng shui* help my pet?

"Feng" (Water)　　　　　　　"Shui" (Wind)

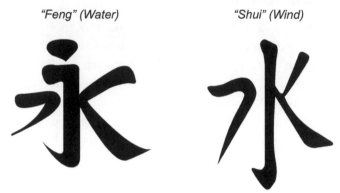

These two elements flow freely around your pet.

As you have the seen in this book, your life is controlled by an invisible life force called *chi*. *Feng shui* is a scientifically proven way to help direct *chi* in a manner that is advantageous to a living organism. From pets to humans, *feng shui* has tremendous powers to help in areas of prosperity, health, and balance. Because all people are manipulated and change with different energy, you see that these manipulations of energy can greatly enhance your pet's life. Your pet can greatly benefit from *feng shui* because the environment is changed or manipulated to help harvest the energy for well-being. There are a lot of misnomers about *feng shui*, such as that it is a religion or is an interior-decorating idea. These assumptions are false. Objects are constantly being placed in your pet's environment and you need to think about how they will affect your pet's personal energy. Eastern philosophy and study have proven that time and time again *feng shui* works not just for humans but also for all living organisms. *Feng shui* influences your pet's life on a daily basis and over the course of a lifetime.

What kind of pet should I get?
What breed?

This is a question I am asked frequently. To answer it, I must ask the prospective pet owner some questions of my own: What kind of companionship are you looking for? Are you looking for a pet that you can walk and physically interact with, or are you looking for a pet that is more independent?

Animals also come in an astonishing range of sizes, and each one presents an equally astonishing range of individual requirements. There are many kinds of animals that make great pets, and each animal group offers many breeds from which to choose. Each breed has certain characteristics that may or may not match up with your personal criteria. Before you bring any animal into your world, consider the major personal commitment that your decision entails … and be sure you can meet the animal's needs.

Dogs need daily walks and physical and mental stimulation in order to be balanced and well adjusted. They need a suitable place to play, to harness their energy, and to share their energy and unconditional love with human companions. Do some research to identify the traits of the dog breed (whether purebred or mixed) that you're considering. If you spend a good amount of time with the dog before acquiring it, you can make a reasonable judgment about its disposition. Once you have made your choice and found a good match, you will have an easier time determining the right dog for you in the future.

Cats do not usually need as much attention in the form of walks, but like dogs, they also need physical and mental energy outlets. You can get a good idea of a cat's disposition during the first meeting.

The other pets you may choose include horses (farm pets), reptiles, birds, and "pocket pets" like guinea pigs, ferrets, hamsters, rats, and mice. As with cats and dogs, you should try to spend some one-on-one time with the animal you're considering bringing into your world.

A final thought: Baby animals are very cute, and you may fall in love with them, but please remember that adopting any pet is a commitment for the pet's *entire* lifetime, even after the animal stops being adorable. Spend some time with a grownup of the same species and breed and ask yourself: Am I willing to commit to spending years with this animal?

My pet's having trouble getting pregnant. What should I do?

Consult a qualified acupuncture practitioner and ask for help. The Appendix can point you to a practitioner in your area.

Acupuncture treatment can yield dramatic, positive results for breeders and others who are looking for help in promoting pet fertility. Before you embark on such a course of treatment, however, you should consider *whether it makes sense* for your pet to get pregnant in the first place. Can you care properly for the new pets you will help to bring into the world, and are you prepared to assume that responsibility? Would it be better to adopt a pet who needs help now? (See the next question.)

Should I adopt a pet, or breed an animal I already have?

Somewhere, there is an animal that deserves the joy and comfort you could provide.

The answer to this question depends on a number of different factors, including why you would choose to breed the animal in the first place, the space and resources you are able to devote to the pet, whether you want a specific kind of animal, and whether or not you are willing to care for and commit to an animal for a lifetime. If you are breeding in order to better the breed, then I would say breeding is a good option. On the other hand, if you are breeding simply to bring a bunch of puppies into the house so that your kids can choose the best of the litter and then send the rest to the pound, you should ask yourself whether adopting might be the more responsible course. There are plenty of good animals to adopt, and adding to the population of pets who need to be placed elsewhere (by bringing five puppies into the world when you are only capable of caring for one) is probably not the best ethical choice.

If you adopt a pet, be sure that it has a full physical examination by a qualified veterinarian before you finalize the adoption. You should know ahead of time about any physical problems. Sometimes a person visits a local shelter and adopts a pet who is sick but does not show any obvious physical symptoms, and then never tries to adopt again because he or she assumes that all animals in shelters are likely to present similar problems. You can avoid such difficulties by setting up your pet adoption through a local animal-rescue group that quarantines sick animals and only offers healthy animals for adoption. Find one in your area by visiting http://www.petfinder.com/shelters.html.

Do you recommend that I spay or neuter my pet?

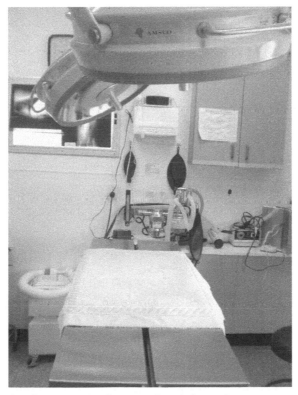

Sterilization procedures can be performed on an outpatient basis.

This is the owner's choice. Many practitioners of Eastern medicine may reject the idea of spaying and neutering pets, but I try to take a balanced approach depending on the larger picture for each pet owner. Due to socioeconomic issues in a culture, there are some situations where a pet owner's decision to neuter or spay a pet makes sense. There can be a problem with unintended pregnancies of animals that get outdoors. If you do decide to spay or neuter your pet, be sure to follow up with good medical care afterward to promote healthy *chi* flow.

What's the maximum number of pets I should have in my home?

Some pets adapt better than others to a multiple-animal household setting.

My experience is that a medium-sized home can accommodate three or perhaps four pets at the most—if the family is willing to invest the time necessary to carefully plan the way they're going to live with their pets.

The layout of the house is a big issue. Pets simply don't like clutter or closed-in spaces, and don't respond well to environments that ask them to adapt to these kinds of problems. If they're forced to live in a space that isn't big enough to accommodate them, they may act out by urinating on the floor or on furniture, or may find other ways to let it be known that they are not happy with the living space situation. Pets who are forced into crowded or poorly designed living spaces may begin fighting with one another, and food aggression is common in these situations as well. If you want more than one pet in your living space, ask yourself: Is the layout of this home really feasible for two, three, or four pets? The layout could be fine while you have kittens or puppies to deal with, but as the animals grow into adults it may become more obvious that you don't really have enough room for your animals to live together harmoniously. Bear in mind that there are no boundary issues for a baby animal ... but that changes once the animal's body size becomes larger. If the environment contains imbalance and the owner doesn't pay attention to it, the imbalance can cycle through different animals in the home, and the dynamics between the pets who once "got along with no problem" could change quickly. It's not at all uncommon for animals to be anxious and aggressive when a pet owner misunderstands the territory and boundary issues, and has not given the animals enough space. Often these pet owners will come to me complaining about a pet's "forgetting" about basic housebreaking issues. The pet hasn't forgotten anything. It's attempting to communicate!

When the adult pets in a living environment are not stressed or antagonistic toward each other, and are not acting out, that's an indication that the living space is in balance.

The worst-case scenario, of course, is the situation where there are dozens of pets in a single living space that clearly can't accommodate them. This indicates a hoarding mentality on the part of the pet owner. This is a human disorder and a human psychological problem. It's a compulsive activity, like collecting newspapers or constantly washing one's hands. Hoarding pets is not healthy for anyone, and certainly not for the pets. Hoarding always brings with it major sanitary problems that present health and safety concerns for both animals and humans.

Hoarders often use the excuse, "No one but me can give these pets the care they need," but the truth, in all of these situations, usually turns out to be that the level of care deteriorates rapidly over time. Simply keeping the living area clean can become a job that takes more time than there are hours in a day. Unfortunately, people who hoard animals tend to hoard more animals as time goes on; they think they are giving good care to the animals, but in fact they're making a bad situation worse.

If you or someone you know is facing a situation where animals are in stress and/or danger because of a hoarding problem, the right response is for the hoarding pet owner to seek psychological help.

My indoor cat now wants to go outdoors. What should I do?

Indoor or outdoor?

If an indoor cat must deal with excessive clutter or a lack of appropriate physical space in your shared living environment, you should not be too surprised if the animal tries to look for new space outside. Indoor cats can and do transition to being outdoor cats, but you may want to start the process by taking the cat out for walks on a harness until it learns to navigate outdoor spaces safely.

While it's true that many cats are happier spending some part of the day outside of their owners' homes than being indoors, it's important to note that this does not relieve you of responsibilities for your cat. You still need to feed and care for your cat, and your cat still needs a litter box, whether or not it's spending a significant amount of time outdoors. Don't make the care, feeding, and droppings of your cat the neighbor's business!

I think an animal in my locality is being abused. What should I do?

If you believe you are a witness to animal abuse, you should report it as soon as possible to the local chapter of the Humane Society or the American Society for the Prevention of Cruelty to Animals (ASPCA). You can find out how to get in touch with responsible people in your area by visiting the Websites http://hsus.org or aspca.org.

Signs of animal abuse might be open sores or wounds, or other physical symptoms such as thinness or *alopecia* (mange). Another all-too-common example of abuse is the dog who is left out for long periods of time in the middle of the yard, chained to a post, with no shelter. Of course, all pets need a clean source of food and water and a clean living area; if you are concerned that an animal in your locality is being deprived of these things, you should call for help. The animal should not be living perpetually in its own waste. Its shelter area should be cleaned on a daily basis. You can—and should—call the Humane Society or the ASPCA for help if you spot an animal that appears to have no one caring for it.

My pet probably doesn't have long to live—so why should I bother with treatment? Shouldn't I just "put the pet down"?

Unfortunately, I get this question a lot. It reflects our society's prevailing belief that pets who are ill are more or less disposable commodities, like disposable cameras or plastic plates.

You should "invest" in the treatment of a dying pet for the same reason you would "invest" in the treatment of a loved one with cancer or kidney problems or any other serious human ailment: because you are eager to improve the quality of the loved one's remaining time with you. Often, there is still the possibility to keep an animal from suffering needlessly, and to make the most of the pet's remaining time by making the pet as comfortable as possible.

Sometimes I have to remind pet owners of the hundreds of hours of companionship, emotional support, and loyalty they've received from their pets. I ask them to think about how long their pet has been part of their life. If you've had your pet for say, five years, don't you think that your pet deserves something back from you during the last year of its own life? Your pet has given you five years of love and companionship. Doesn't it make sense and isn't it common "human" decency to make an effort to give something back to your pet by making him as comfortable as possible for as long as possible?

If you love your pet, know your pet well, and find yourself in a position to make decisions that will affect his final passage, ask yourself this question: *If my pet were the human and if I were the animal who was suffering, what decision would my pet make?*

Why can't you prolong my pet's life?

This is the opposite side of the question I just examined. Here, instead of a pet owner wondering how quickly he or she can "put the animal down," the pet owner wants to know why the veterinarian can't extend a beloved pet's life at will. Interestingly, I often get this question from the very same pet owners who initially wanted to limit their "investment" in a pet who is experiencing serious illness!

It's actually quite understandable that people should experience this progression. Initially, a pet owner is skeptical that anything can be done for a terminally ill pet; perhaps a traditional Western veterinary approach has led the pet owner to believe that the best thing for the animal is to "put it to sleep." Then the pet owner learns that there are other treatment options that incorporate Eastern medicine and can significantly improve the pet's quality of life, and can result in months or even years of additional quality time with the pet. Having experienced that benefit, when the pet owner begins to see the animal decline, it's natural to ask: *Why does it have to end? Isn't there something else you can do?*

This is the Chinese character for Eternity.

It's good to remember here that veterinarians are doctors; we aren't miracle workers. Pets, like people, have a certain capacity within their system for life. There is only a certain amount of life within each body; Eastern medicine, Western medicine, or a combination of the two can only extend what is already there. The right treatment can maximize what the pet already has; it cannot create new life from scratch.

Some animals simply live longer than others due to genetics, diet, or living conditions. It's important to understand that a veterinarian cannot magically add years to any pet's life—even though the vet wishes he or she could, and even though the veterinarian can understand why pet owners may come to believe that vets can do this. What vets *can* sometimes do is maximize the pet's life potential, just as a human being tries to make the most of his or her own talents, skills, or capacities.

The cases that cause me the most personal regret as a physician are the ones where the pet owners put off reaching out to me for help, and then call me near the end of a pet's life cycle, asking to bestow another year to a beloved pet's life. In these situations, I can only tell the pet owner that I will do what I can, which is usually not as much as either of us would like.

The moral here is simple: Reach out early! Ask for help early! Get a second opinion when you *first* hear that your pet has a serious health problem!

When is the right time to euthanize a pet?

Only the pet owner can answer this question. As a veterinarian, when I feel an animal is suffering and I know that I cannot do anything about that suffering, I tell the owner that we've reached that point, and then let the pet owner make the difficult decision about whether we should euthanize the pet.

Some people have religious beliefs that specify that they cannot euthanize a pet under any circumstances. My feeling is that these people may not realize how much pain they are putting their animal through. Other pet owners, as you have seen, may be too receptive to the prevailing notion that the moment to "put the animal down" is almost immediately after it becomes clear that the animal is terminally ill. These pet owners may want to take a more balanced approach to the question, as well.

The process of euthanasia can be very caring and supportive when it's performed by an experienced and empathetic practitioner.

How should I dispose of my pet's remains?

This, too, is a personal matter.

There are several choices available for handling pet remains; you should discuss them with your veterinarian who can point you toward responsible local people who will handle this for you.

- One option is to have your pet cremated so that you can have the ashes as a reminder of your pet's time with you.
- Another, more expensive option is to bury your pet in a pet cemetery.
- A third option is group cremation; in this scenario, there are no ashes to take home, but the pet owner knows that the remains have been disposed of in a responsible way.

My feeling is that veterinarians should lay out these options for pet owners and let them decide on their own, without pushing the owner in any one of these directions. After a pet owner has made that decision, I like to give him or her a special candle in memory of the pet who just passed, and as an acknowledgment from me, on a personal level, of the emotional difficulty of losing a beloved friend.

Epilogue

In dwelling, live close to the ground. In thinking, keep to the simple. In conflict, be fair and generous. In governing, don't try to control. In work, do what you enjoy. In family life, be completely present.

—Tao Te Ching (*Classical Chinese text*)

I know I've given you a great deal to think about in this book. I don't expect you to master all of the concepts I've shared with you right away, but I do want to close with some simple advice that I think each and every pet owner reading this book can implement instantly:

Treat your pets as the family members they are, and try to be completely present in all your interactions with them.

Just as your children, parents, grandparents, and great-grandparents teach you important lessons about your own passage in this life, your pet has much to share with you on this score. When you welcome a pet into your life, I believe you should do so with the same respect, acceptance, and love that you reserve for those to whom you are closest in this life. You begin your own life's journey as an infant, and make your way through various stages, noting as you go that those whom you love are making their own journeys through their own stages. Nothing is static. Everything is changing. When you look closely at the lives of family members, you see constant reminders of the fragility, and the brevity, of your own journey through this life. It is my privilege to work with animals and humans who have adopted *each other* as nothing less than family members, and who are helping and supporting each other along the way in that remarkable shared journey. To be fully present during that journey, even for a moment, is to recognize its essential sacredness.

As I close, I wish you and the animals in your life many such moments.

Appendix

Alternative Veterinary Practitioners

The following doctors and animal hospitals are part of the global network of holistic practitioners and have expressed an openness to alternative approaches to veterinary medicine. Each has a unique background and unique insights; check with the veterinarian in your area to determine the specific treatment options offered so you can make the best choice for your pet. The appearance of a listing in this Appendix is in no way an endorsement of any doctor or hospital; this list is merely a summary of resources for evaluation by pet owners.

Of course, you can always reach out to me:

Stacy H. Fuchino, VMD

P.V. Pet Hospital Veterinary Services

Redondo Beach, California, 90277

310-375-6811

www.pvpet.com

Websites of Interest

Alternative Medicine for Pets: www.altvetmed.com

American Holistic Veterinary Medical Association: www.ahvma.org

Marty Goldstein, DVM: www.drmarty.com

The following care providers may also be of interest if you are looking for practitioners in your area.

Alabama

HOLISTIC VETERINARY MEDICAL CENTER OF ALABAMA, Eclectic, Alabama, http://web.me.com/marybdvm/hvmca/home.html

BELTLINE ANIMAL HOSPITAL, Mobile, Alabama, www.dogtorj.com

TLC VETERINARY HOSPITAL, Semmes, Alabama, www.yourtlcvet.net

Alaska

THE PET STOP, Anchorage, Alaska, www.petstopak.com

Arizona

ALL PETS ACUPUNCTURE & HOLISTIC HEALTH CLINIC, Cornville, Arizona, www.apahvet.com

VET ON WHEELS, Fountain Hills, Arizona, www.vetonwheels.net

ANTHEM PET MEDICAL CENTER, Phoenix, Arizona, www.anthempetcare.com

HARMONY VETERINARY CARE, Prescott, Arizona, www.harmonyvetcare.com

INA ROAD ANIMAL HOSPITAL, Tucson, Arizona, www.inaroadanimalhospital.com

PARTNERS IN ANIMAL WELLNESS SERVICES (P.A.W.S.), Tucson, Arizona, www.pawstucson.com

Arkansas

DR. PAT BRADLEY, Conway, Arkansas, www.drpatbradley.com

California

HOLISTIC VETERINARY CENTER, Calabasas, California, www.holistic-vet-center.com

CARDIFF ANIMAL HOSPITAL, Cardiff, California, www.cardiffanimalhospital.com

HEALING SPIRIT ANIMAL WELLNESS CENTER, Eureka, California, www.healingspiritvet.com

VCA ALL CARE ANIMAL REFERRAL CENTER, Fountain Valley, California, www.robertwoodsdvm.com

ABBY PET HOSPITAL, Fresno, California, www.abbypethospital.com

HEMOPET, Garden Grove, California, www.hemopet.org

EVERGLO-NATURAL™ VETERINARY SERVICES, INC., Gualala, California, www.holisticvetpetcare.net

CENTINELA ANIMAL HOSPITAL, Inglewood, California, www.lovapet.com

IRVINE VETERINARY SERVICES, Irvine, California, www.irvinevetservices.com

ALL CREATURES VETERINARY CARE CENTER, La Quinta, California, www.laquintavet.com

VCA ARROYO ANIMAL HOSPITAL, Lake Forest, California, www.vcaarroyo.com

LONG BEACH ANIMAL HOSPITAL, Long Beach, California, www.lbah.com

ELLA BITTEL, DVM (SPIRITS IN TRANSITION), Los Alamos, California, www.spiritsintransition.org

ANIMAL SPECIALTY GROUP, Los Angeles, California, www.asgvets.com

HOLISTIC VETERINARY HEALTHCARE, Los Angeles, California, www.theholisticvet.com

ANIMAL & BIRD CLINIC OF MISSION VIEJO, Mission Viejo, California, www.abcofmv.vetsuite.com

ACUPUNCTURE FOR PETS, Newbury Park, California, www.acupuncture4pets.net

THE COUNTRY VET, Novato, California, www.thecountryvet.com

CREATURE COMFORT HOLISTIC VETERINARY CENTER, Oakland, California, www.creaturecomfort.com

HOLISTIC VETERINARY CARE, Oakland, California, www.holisticvetcare.com

COASTAL HOLISTIC COMPLEMENTARY VETERINARY SERVICES, Pacifica, California, www.coastalholistic.com

INTEGRATIVE VETERINARY CENTER, Sacramento, California, www.integrativeveterinarycenter.com

THE PET WHISPERER (DR. BLAKE CONSULTING), San Diego, California, www.thepetwhisperer.com

SOUTH SAN DIEGO VETERINARY HOSPITAL, San Diego, California, www.ssdpetvet.com

THE WESTERN DRAGON INTEGRATED VETERINARY SOLUTIONS, San Jose, California, www.thewesterndragon.com

HOLISTIC VETERINARY HOUSE CALL SERVICES, San Leandro, California, www.holisticpetvet.net

ALL PETS VETERINARY CLINIC, Santa Cruz, California, www.vetgateglobal.com

THE ACADEMY OF VETERINARY HOMEOPATHY, Santa Rosa, California, www.theavh.org

CODDINGTOWN VETERINARY CLINIC, Santa Rosa, California, www.coddingtownvet.com

DEBORAH MATHIS, DVM, Saratoga, California, www.5elementvet.com/Alternative_Veterinary_Medicine/Home.html

VCA FORESTVILLE VETERINARY HOSPITAL, Sebastopol, California, www.vca.com

HEALING HOPE, Solana Beach, California, www.healinghope.net

ALTERNATIVE VETERINARY CARE, Soquel, California, www.animalmagic.us

ALTERNATIVE VETERINARY MEDICINE AND KENNELS, South Lake Tahoe, California, www.drkostecki.com

HOLISTIC ANIMAL DOCTOR (Audra MacCorkle, DVM), Sun Valley, California, www.drmaccorkle.com

LIMEHOUSE VETERINARY CLINIC, Toluca Lake, California, www.limehousevet.com

NORTH TUSTIN VETERINARY CLINIC, Tustin, California, www.robertwoodsdvm.com

VALLEY VETERINARY HOSPITAL, Walnut Creek, California, www.valleyvethosp.com

CACHE CREEK HOLISTIC VETERINARY SERVICE, Woodland, California, www.cchvs.com

Colorado

ASPEN ANIMAL HOSPITAL, Aspen, Colorado, www.aspenanimalhospital.com

BOULDER'S NATURAL ANIMAL, Boulder, Colorado, www.bouldersnaturalanimal.com

ELEMENTAL EQUINE SERVICES, LLC, Brighton, Colorado, www.elementalequineservices.com

PEAK PERFORMANCE VETERINARY GROUP, Colorado Springs, Colorado, www.peakvets.com

HOLISTIC CARE FOR ANIMALS, Denver, Colorado, www.holisticcareforanimals.com

LANCASTER VETERINARY SERVICES, Denver, Colorado, www.lisavet.com

ACUVET (Certified Veterinary Acupuncture), Englewood, Colorado, www.acuvethealing.com

BELLEVIEW ANIMAL CLINIC, Englewood, Colorado, www.belleviewanimalclinic.com

COLORADO STATE UNIVERSITY (College of Veterinary Medicine and Biomedical Sciences), Fort Collins, Colorado, www.csuvets.colostate.edu/pain

HARMONY ANIMAL WELLNESS, Kittredge, Colorado, www.harmonyanimalwellness.com

CHAPARRAL ANIMAL HEALTH CENTER, Longmont, Colorado, www.wellvet.com

MORNINGSTAR VETERINARY CLINIC, Montrose, Colorado, www.morningstarvet.com

PET KARE CLINIC, Steamboat Springs, Colorado, www.petkareclinic.com

Connecticut

ANIMAL HEALTH PRACTICE and EQUINE HEALTH PRACTICE, Bantam, Connecticut, www.animalhealthpractice.com

ANNE C. HERMANS, DVM, Bridgewater, Connecticut, www.vethomeopath.com

FRONTIER MEDICINE, East Granby, Connecticut, www.frontiervetmed.com

BECKETT AND ASSOCIATES VETERINARY SERVICES, LLC, Glastonbury, Connecticut, www.beckettvet.net

ALLEN M. SCHOEN, DVM, MS, & ASSOCIATES, LLC, Sherman, Connecticut, www.drschoen.com

HEALING CENTER FOR ANIMALS, Westport, Connecticut, www.healingcenterforanimals.com

SCHULHOF ANIMAL HOSPITAL, Westport, Connecticut, www.schulhofanimalhospital.com

Delaware

COMPANION ANIMAL PRACTICE, Smyrna, Delaware, www.companionanimalpractice.com

WILMINGTON ANIMAL HOSPITAL, Wilmington, Delaware, www.wilmingtonanimalhospital.com

District of Columbia

MERIDIAN VETERINARY SERVICES, Washington, D. C.,
www.meridianpet.com

Florida

WILNER VETERINARY CONSULT (phone consultations only),
Fort Lauderdale, Florida, www.wilnerveterinaryconsult.com

MIDWAY ANIMAL ALTERNATIVE AND
COMPLEMENTARY CLINIC, Homosassa, Florida, www.dr-trish.com

ANIMAL CLINIC OF IVES DAIRY ROAD, Miami, Florida,
(305) 653-3939

LUDLAM–DIXIE ANIMAL CLINIC, Miami, Florida,
www.naturalpetdoc.com

NATURAL HOLISTIC HEALTH CARE, Miami, Florida,
www.naturalholistic.com

ROBERT PANE, DVM, (AT SOUTH KENDALL ANIMAL
HOSPITAL), Miami, Florida, www.southkendall.com

ANIMAL HEALTH OASIS VETERINARY SERVICE, Naples,
Florida, www.animalhealthoasis.com

ANIMAL & BIRD MEDICAL CENTER OF PALM HARBOR,
Palm Harbor, Florida, www.pethealing.org

PAMPERED PET HEALTH CENTER, Port Charlotte, Florida,
www.pamperedpet.petplace.com

COASTAL ANIMAL HOSPITAL WELLNESS CENTER,
Rockledge, Florida, www.coastalanimalhospitalrockledge.com

INTEGRATIVE ANIMAL MEDICAL CENTER, Sarasota,
Florida, www.holisticanimalcare.com

HOMEOPATHY FOR ANIMALS, Stuart, Florida,
www.homeopathyanimals.com

STUART ANIMAL HOSPITAL, Stuart, Florida,
www.stuartanimalhospital.com

OAKWOOD ANIMAL HOSPITAL AND WELLNESS CLINIC,
Tallahassee, Florida, www.oakwoodanimal.com

RUSSELL SWIFT, DVM (THE RIGHT REMEDY), Tamarac, Florida, www.therightremedy.com

ANIMAL ALTERNATIVES HOLISTIC HEALTH CARE CLINIC, Tampa, Florida, www.animalalternatives.org

CEDAR BAY VETERINARY CLINIC, Winter Garden, Florida, www.cedarbayvet.com

Georgia

ATLANTA HOLISTIC VETERINARY CARE, Atlanta, Georgia, www.atlantaholisticveterinarycare.com

VCA LILBURN ANIMAL HOSPITAL, Lilburn, Georgia, www.vcahospitals.com/lilburn

GEORGIA VETERINARY SPECIALISTS, Sandy Springs, Georgia, www.susanwynn.com

GWINNETT ANIMAL HOSPITAL, Snellville, Georgia, www.gwinnettanimalhospital.com

Hawaii

ALL CREATURES GREAT & SMALL, Kapaa, Kauai, Hawaii, www.drbasko.com

KAPA'AU VETERINARY CENTER, Kapa'au, Hawaii, www.kapaauveterinarycenter.com

Idaho

ANIMAL HEALTH HOSPITAL, Boise, Idaho, (208) 562-0156

AULTERNATIVES, Nampa, Idaho, www.aulternatives.com

Illinois

NATURAL PET ANIMAL HOSPITAL, Bourbonnais, Illinois, www.drkarenbecker.com

HOLISTIC VETERINARIAN (JUDITH SWANSON, DVM), Chicago, Illinois, www.4mfg.net/drswanson/

INTEGRATIVE PET CARE, Chicago, Illinois,
www.integrativepetcare.com

ROYAL TREATMENT VETERINARY SPA, Chicago, Illinois,
www.royaltreatmentvetspa.com

CHICAGO ANIMAL REHAB, Chicago Ridge, Illinois,
www.chicagoanimalrehab.com

RISING SUN VETERINARY CLINIC, Des Plaines, Illinois,
www.risingsunvetclinic.com

ARBORETUM VIEW ANIMAL HOSPITAL, Downers Grove,
Illinois, www.avah.org

ELBURN ANIMAL HOSPITAL, Elburn, Illinois,
www.elburnanimalhospital.com

LE PAR ANIMAL HOSPITAL, Evergreen Park, Illinois,
www.leparvet.com

TOPS VETERINARY REHAB, Grayslake, Illinois,
www.tops-vet-rehab.com

CANINE SPORTS MEDICINE CENTER, Lake Villa, Illinois,
www.k9sportmed.com

NESS EXOTIC WELLNESS CENTER, Lisle, Illinois,
www.nessexotic.com

SKYCREST ANIMAL CLINIC, Long Grove, Illinois,
www.skycrestvet.com

RICHMOND VETERINARY CLINIC, Richmond, Illinois,
www.rvetclinic.com

KNOLLWOOD HOSPITAL FOR PETS, Schaumburg, Illinois,
www.knollwoodhospitalforpets.com

ANIMAL HOSPITAL OF GURNEE, Wadsworth, Illinois,
www.ahog.us

Indiana

THE PAW PATCH PLACE ANIMAL HOSPITAL, Indianapolis,
Indiana, www.pawpatchplace.com

PET PALS VETERINARY HOSPITAL AND HOUSECALLS,
Indianapolis, Indiana, www.petpalsveterinaryhospital.com

NOBLESVILLE VETERINARY CLINIC, Noblesville, Indiana, www.noblesvillevetclinic.com

HOOFSTOCK VETERINARY SERVICE, Pine Village, Indiana, http://hoofstockvet.com

SOUTHLANE VETERINARY HOSPITAL, Valparaiso, Indiana, www.southlanevet.com

Iowa

IOWA VETERINARY ACUPUNCTURE CLINIC, Des Moines, Iowa, www.apvet.com

NATURAL SOLUTIONS, Des Moines, Iowa, www.naturalsolutionsforpets.com

FAIRFIELD ANIMAL HOSPITAL, Fairfield, Iowa, www.healthyvet.com

RICHARD HOLLIDAY, DVM, Waukon, Iowa, www.rjhollidaydvm.com

Kansas

ARBOR CREEK ANIMAL HOSPITAL, Olathe, Kansas, www.acanimalhospital.com

ACUPUNCTURE AND HERBS FOR PETS, Kansas City and Prairie Village, Kansas, www.westonvet.com

METCALF SOUTH ANIMAL HOSPITAL, Overland Park, Kansas, www.metcalfsouthanimalhospital.com

Kentucky

ALL PAWS VET SERVICES, Lebanon, Kentucky, www.allpaws.us

HEALING HANDS PET ACUPUNCTURE, Louisville, Kentucky, www.healinghandspet.com

HORIZON VETERINARY SERVICES, Simpsonville, Kentucky, www.horizonvetserv.com

Louisiana

ALTERNATIVE VETERINARY CLINIC, Gretna, Louisiana, (504) 393-6400

Maine

FULL CIRCLE HOLISTIC VETERINARY CLINIC, Belfast, Maine, www.fullcircleholisticvet.com

BETHEL ANIMAL HOSPITAL, Bethel, Maine, www.bethelanimalhospital.com

HOLISTIC HEALING FOR ANIMALS, Yarmouth, Maine, www.holistichealingforanimals.net

Maryland

VETERINARY HOLISTIC CARE, Bethesda, Maryland, www.vhcdoc.com

JENNIFER RAMMELMEIER, DVM (VETERINARY HOLISTIC HOUSECALLS), Clarksville, Maryland, www.holisticdvm.com

ANIMAL WELLNESS CENTER, Columbia, Maryland, www.acuvet.com

COMPASSIONATE VETERINARY HOUSECALLS, Columbia, Maryland, www.compassionatehomevet.com

SOUTH ARUNDEL VETERINARY HOSPITAL, Edgewater, Maryland, www.southarundelvet.com

ANIMAL CARE CENTER, Joppa, Maryland, www.myanimalcarecenter.com/index.htm

BAYSIDE ANIMAL MEDICAL CENTER, Severna Park, Maryland, www.baysideanimal.com

CHRISTINA CHAMBREAU, DVM, Sparks, Maryland, www.christinachambreau.com

Massachusetts

THE CAT DOCTOR, Bedford and Nashua, Massachusetts, www.catdoctors.com

SLADE VETERINARY HOSPITAL, Framingham, Massachusetts, www.sladevet.com

M.A.S.H. (MAIN STREET ANIMAL SERVICES OF HOPKINTON), Hopkinton, Massachusetts, www.mashvet.com

KINGSTON ANIMAL HOSPITAL, Kingston, Massachusetts, www.healthyveterinaryalternatives.com

WINDY HOLLOW VETERINARY CLINIC, Montague, Massachusetts, www.windyhollowvet.com

ALTERNATIVE VETERINARY SERVICES, North Andover, Massachusetts, www.altvetservices.com

LANDAU VETERINARY SERVICES, Pelham, Massachusetts, www.landauvet.com

FIREHOUSE VETERINARY CLINIC, Plymouth, Massachusetts, www.firehousevet.com

PARKWAY VETERINARY HOSPITAL, West Roxbury, Massachusetts, www.parkwayvethospital.com

Michigan

OAKLAND VETERINARY REFERRAL SERVICES, Bloomfield Hills, Michigan, www.ovrs.com

SOUTH CROSSING VETERINARY CENTER, Caledonia, Michigan, www.southcrossingvet.com

COMPANION ANIMAL CARE CORNER, Caro, Michigan, www.drgalka.com

WOODSIDE ANIMAL CLINIC, Royal Oak, Michigan, www.doc4pets.com

VETERINARY GENERAL, Shelby Township, Michigan, www.veterinarygeneral.com

BEST FRIENDS PET WELLNESS, Willis, Michigan, www.bestfriendspetwellness.com

Minnesota

WHOLE HEALTH VETERINARY, Blaine, Minnesota, www.wholehealthvet.com

ANIMAL WELLNESS CENTER, Lakeville, Minnesota, www.altpetvet.com

LAKE HARRIET VETERINARY, Minneapolis, Minnesota, www.lakeharrietvet.com

PEQUOT LAKES ANIMAL HOSPITAL, Pequot Lakes, Minnesota, www.pequotlakesanimalhospital.com

UNIVERSITY OF MINNESOTA COLLEGE OF VETERINARY MEDICINE, St. Paul, Minnesota, www.cvm.umn.edu

Mississippi

ALTERNATIVE VETERINARY CARE, Brandon, Mississippi, (601) 919-3566

Missouri

CANINE PERFORMANCE MEDICINE, Lees Summit, Missouri, www.canineperformancemed.com

VETERINARY ALTERNATIVES, Peculiar, Missouri, www.vetalternatives.com

ANIMAL HEALTH & HEALING, St. Louis, Missouri, www.animalhealthandhealing.com

ACUPUNCTURE AND HERBS FOR PETS, Weston, Missouri, www.westonvet.com

Montana

CIRCLE OF LIFE ANIMAL WELLNESS CENTER, Billings, Montana, www.circleoflifeawc.com

Nevada

ANIMAL KINGDOM VETERINARY HOSPITAL, Las Vegas, Nevada, www.holistic-veterinarian.com

NATURAL CARE INSTITUTE, Las Vegas, Nevada, www.naturalcareinstitute.com

LAKESIDE ANIMAL HOSPITAL, Reno, Nevada, www.lakesideanimalhospital.com

New Hampshire

HOLISTIC VETERINARY CENTER, Concord, New Hampshire, www.holisticvetcenter.com

HEALTH AND WELLNESS ANIMAL HOSPITAL OF HAMPTON FALLS, Hampton Falls, New Hampshire, www.healthandwellnessanimalhospital.com

DR. DAN'S INTEGRATIVE PET HOSPTIAL, Hudson, New Hampshire, www.drdandvm.com

EQUINE WELLNESS (JACQUELINE DEDEO LOWE, DVM), Milford, New Hampshire, www.equinewellnessne.com

New Jersey

CLAYTON VETERINARY ASSOCIATES, Clayton, New Jersey, www.claytonvetnj.com

COLTS NECK ANIMAL CLINIC, Colts Neck, New Jersey, www.homeovet.com

HILLSDALE ANIMAL HOSPITAL, Hillsdale, New Jersey, www.healingvet.com

HOLISTIC PET CARE, Little Falls, New Jersey, www.hpcnj.com

LIVINGSTON ANIMAL HOSPITAL, Livingston, New Jersey, www.livingstonvet.com

MARGATE ANIMAL HOSPITAL AND ALTERNATIVE CARE CENTER, Margate, New Jersey, www.alternativevet.com

THREE RIVERS HOLISTIC VETERINARY SERVICES, Morristown, New Jersey, www.njholisticvet.com

CLASSIC VETERINARY HOMEOPATHY (CEDARBROOK ANIMAL HOSPITAL), Sicklerville, New Jersey, www.canineworld.com/drdym

VETERINARY ACUPUNCTURE SERVICES, Sparta, New Jersey, www.drlounsberry.com

New Mexico

ANIMAL ACUPUNCTURE VET, Santa Fe, New Mexico, www.animalacupuncturevet.com

LOS ANIMALES HOLISTIC VETERINARY CARE AND EDUCATION (DEE BLANCO, DVM), Santa Fe, New Mexico, www.drdeeblanco.com

New York

VETERINARY ACUPUNCTURE AND HEALING ARTS, Ardsley and Long Island, New York, www.longislandholisticveterinarian.com

KNOLL'S END ANIMAL HOSPITAL, Berkshire, New York, www.knollsend.com

THE VET AT THE BARN, Chestnut Ridge, New York, www.vetatthebarn.com

HALFMOON VETERINARY HOSPITAL (VETERINARY WELLNESS CENTER), Clifton Park, New York, www.holisticpetcaretoday.com

BROOKVILLE ANIMAL HOSPITAL, Glen Head, New York, brookvilleanimal.com

ANIMAL WELLNESS CENTER, Huntington, New York, www.animalwellness.net

COLONIAL VETERINARY HOSPITAL, Ithaca, New York, www.colonialvet.com

ANIMAL CLINIC OF LONG ISLAND CITY, Long Island City, New York, www.longislandanimalclinic.com

MACEDON VETERINARY CARE, Macedon, New York, www.macedonvetcare.com

PETMEND ANIMAL HOSPITAL, Mamaroneck, New York, www.petmend.com

ANIMAL ACUPUNCTURE (BABETTE GLADSTEIN, DVM), New York, New York, www.animalacupuncture.net

EAST MEETS WEST VETERINARY CARE, New York, New York, www.eastwestvetcare.com

HOUSE CALLS FOR YOUR PET, New York, New York, www.housecallsforyourpet.com

RITZY CANINE CARRIAGE HOUSE, New York, New York, www.ritzycanine.com/index.htm

PLEASANT VALLEY ANIMAL HOSPITAL, Pleasant Valley, New York, www.pleasantvalleyveterinary.com

BLOOMINGROVE VETERINARY HOSPITAL (THE WHOLISTIC VET), Rensselaer, New York, www.thewholisticvet.com

SMITH RIDGE VETERINARY CENTER (MARTIN GOLDSTEIN, DVM), South Salem, New York, www.smithridge.com

PROMOTING ANIMAL WELLNESS, Warwick, New York, www.pamshultzdvm.com

North Carolina

RIVERSONG VETERINARY CLINIC, Brevard, North Carolina, www.riversongvet.com

ATRIUM ANIMAL HOSPITAL, Charlotte, North Carolina, www.atriumanimalhospital.com

BONNIE BRAE VETERINARY HOSPITAL, Columbus, North Carolina, www.bonniebraeveterinaryhospital.com

TRIANGLE VETERINARY HOSPITAL, Durham, North Carolina, www.trianglevet.com

TIMBERCREEK VETERINARY HOSPITAL (THOMAS SCHELL, DVM, DABVP), Jonesville, North Carolina, www.timbercreekvet.com

HOLISTIC VETERINARY SERVICES, Kings Mountain, North Carolina, www.aholisticvet.com

CHARLES LOOPS, DVM, Pittsboro, North Carolina,
www.charlesloopsdvm.com

PERRIN HEARTWAY, DVM, Pittsboro, North Carolina,
www.heartwayholisticvet.com

AVIAN AND EXOTIC ANIMAL CARE, Raleigh, North
Carolina, www.avianandexotic.com

BOWMAN ANIMAL HOSPITAL AND CAT CLINIC, Raleigh,
North Carolina, www.bowmananimalhospital.com

HIDDEN VALLEY ANIMAL HOSPITAL (BRIAN LAPHAM,
DVM), Raleigh, North Carolina, www.drlapham.com

MOUNT TABOR ANIMAL HOSPITAL, Winston-Salem, North
Carolina, www.mtah.net

North Dakota

CASSELTON VETERINARY SERVICE, Casselton, North
Dakota, www.cassvetservice.com

Ohio

VETERINARY ALTERNATIVES, Centerville, Ohio,
www.veterinaryalternatives.com

COUNTY ANIMAL CLINIC, Coldwater, Ohio,
www.animaldoctor.vetsuite.com

LIFETIME PET WELLNESS CENTER, Columbus, Ohio,
www.northworthingtonpetclinic.com

OHIO HOLISTIC VETERINARY SERVICE, Columbus, Ohio,
www.drdonn.com

VETERINARY WELLNESS CENTER, Harrison, Ohio,
www.vetwellness.com

ALL ABOUT PETCARE, Middletown, Ohio,
www.allaboutpetcare.com

HOLISTIC VETERINARY PRACTICE, North Canton, Ohio,
www.holisticvetpractice.com

WELLNESS PATH HOLISTIC VETERINARY CARE, Northfield Center, Ohio, www.wellnesspathvet.com

DANCING PAWS ANIMAL WELLNESS CENTER, Richfield, Ohio, www.dancingpawsawc.com

SYCAMORE ANIMAL HOSPITAL, Sycamore, Ohio, www.sycamoreanimal.com

COUNTRYSIDE ANIMAL HOSPITAL, Sylvania, Ohio, www.countryside-ah.com

Oklahoma

MUSTANG ANIMAL HEALTH CLINIC, Mustang, Oklahoma, www.mustanganimalhealthclinic.com

TERRY WOOD, DVM (MUSTANG VETERINARY HOSPITAL), Mustang, Oklahoma, www.terrywooddvm.com

BEST FRIENDS ANIMAL HOSPITAL, Shawnee, Oklahoma, www.oklahomapethealth.com

ALL PETS VETERINARY HOSPITAL, Stillwater, Oklahoma, www.allpetsvethospital.net

Oregon

SAGE VETERINARY ALTERNATIVES, Bend, Oregon, www.sagevet.com

PAWSITIVE MOTION, Creswell, Oregon, www.pawsitivemotion.com

A PLACE FOR HEALING, Damascus, Oregon, www.donnastarita.com

DOGWOOD PET HOSPITAL, Gresham, Oregon, www.dogwoodpet.com

KINDRED SPIRITS ACUPUNCTURE AND ORIENTAL MEDICINE CLINIC, Lake Oswego, Oregon, www.kindredspiritsacupuncture.com

HAWTHORNE VETERINARY CLINIC, Portland, Oregon, www.hawthornevet.com

TWO RIVERS VET CLINIC, Portland, Oregon, www.tworiversvet.com

CASCADE ANIMAL CLINIC (KELLI ROSEN, DVM), Springfield, Oregon, www.drkellirosen.com/CascadeAnimalClinic.htm

MCKENZIE ANIMAL HOSPITAL, Springfield, Oregon, www.mckenzieanimalhospital.com

HOLISTIC PET VET CLINIC, Tigard, Oregon, www.holisticpetvetclinic.com

CASCADE SUMMIT ANIMAL HOSPITAL, West Linn, Oregon, www.cascadesummitvets.com

Pennsylvania

DOUGLAS KNUEVEN, DVM (BEAVER ANIMAL CLINIC), Beaver, Pennsylvania, www.beaveranimalclinic.com

ANIMAL WELLNESS CENTER, Chadds Ford, Pennsylvania, www.altpetdoc.com

CHESTNUT HILL VETERINARY HOSPITAL, Erdenheim, Pennsylvania, www.chestnuthillvet.com

VETERINARY SPECIALITY AND EMERGENCY CENTER, Langhorne, Pennsylvania, www.vsecvet.com

ALWAYS HELPFUL VETERINARY SERVICES, Nottingham, Pennsylvania, www.judithshoemaker.com

ROCKLEDGE VETERINARY CLINIC, Rockledge, Pennsylvania, www.rockledgevet.com

Rhode Island

WOLF ROCK ANIMAL HEALTH CENTER, Exeter, Rhode Island, www.wolfrockanimals.com

SHARON R. DOOLITTLE DVM, Smithfield, Rhode Island, www.holisticanimalvet.com

South Carolina

AIKEN VETERINARY CLINIC, Aiken, South Carolina,
www.aikenvet.com

EQUINE THERAPEUTIC OPTIONS, Aiken, South Carolina,
www.ultimatesaddlesolutions.com

SUN DOG CAT MOON VETERINARY CLINIC, John's Island,
South Carolina, www.sundogcatmoon.com

ALL ABOUT PETS, Travelers Rest, South Carolina,
www.holisticvetsc.com

Tennessee

FOUR WINDS HOLISTIC ANIMAL SERVICES, Knoxville,
Tennessee, home.earthlink.net/~fourwinds

THE WHOLE POINT (IN-HOME VETERINARY
ACUPUNCTURE), Knoxville, Tennessee, www.wholepointvet.com

Texas

ANTHONY ANIMAL CLINIC AND HOLISTIC HEALING
CENTER, Anthony, Texas, www.anthonyanimalclinic.com

ALTERNATIVES 4 ANIMAL HEALTH, Austin, Texas,
www.alt4animals.com

CRYSTAL MOUNTAIN ANIMAL HOSPITAL, Austin, Texas,
www.vandervet.com

HIWAY 620 ANIMAL HOSPITAL, Austin, Texas,
www.620vet.com

LOVE PET HOSPITAL, Austin, Texas, www.lovepethospital.com

HARWOOD OAKS ANIMAL CLINIC, Bedford, Texas,
www.harwoodoaksanimalclinic.com

ALTERNATIVE VETERINARY HOSPITAL, Carrollton, Texas,
www.alternativeveterinaryhospital.com

KAREN AVE, DVM, (VETERINARY ACPUNCTURE AND
ALTERNATIVE THERAPIES) Carrollton, Texas,
www.animalacuvet.com

VITALITY PETCARE, Dallas, Texas, www.vitalitypetcare.com

VETERANS MEMORIAL DRIVE ANIMAL HOSPITAL, Houston, Texas, www.vmdah.net

PAWS AND CLAWS ANIMAL HOSPITAL (PET CARE NATURALLY), Plano, Texas, www.petcarenaturally.com

COMPASSIONATE CARE VETERINARY SERVICES, San Antonio, Texas, www.holisticpetdoc.com

Utah

DANCING CATS FELINE HEALTH CENTER, Salt Lake City, Utah, www.dancingcatsvet.com

ANIMAL CARE CENTER, West Bountiful, Utah, www.utahanimalcare.com

Vermont

NANCY FIREY, DVM (VERMONT VETERINARY ALTERNATIVES), Jericho, Vermont, www.vtvetalternatives.com

STEPHANIE WOOLWICH-HOLZMAN VMD (DANCING DRAGON ANIMAL HEALTH), Manchester Center, Vermont, www.doctorstephanie.com

COLD RIVER VETERINARY CENTER, North Clarendon, Vermont, www.crvetcenter.com

Virginia

DEL RAY ANIMAL HOSPITAL, Alexandria, Virginia, www.delrayanimalhospital.com

FULL CIRCLE EQUINE SERVICE, Amissville, Virginia, www.fullcircleequine.com

BALLSTON ANIMAL HOSPITAL, Arlington, Virginia, www.ballstonanimalhospital.com

ASHBURN FARM ANIMAL HOSPITAL, Ashburn, Virginia, www.ashburnfarmvet.com

CHARLOTTESVILLE VETERINARY HOSPITAL,
Charlottesville, Virginia, www.charlottesvilleveterinaryhospital.com

COOKE VETERINARY MEDICAL CENTER, Chesapeake,
Virginia, www.cookevet.com

SOUTH PAWS VETERINARY SPECIALISTS AND
EMERGENCY CENTER, Fairfax, Virginia, www.southpaws.com

FALLS CHURCH ANIMAL HOSPITAL, Falls Church, Virginia,
www.fallschurchanimalhospital.com

HARMANY EQUINE CLINIC, Flint Hill, Virginia,
www.harmanyequine.com

GREAT FALLS ANIMAL HOSPITAL, Great Falls, Virginia,
www.greatfallsanimalhospital.com

PEARL VETERINARY HOLISTIC MEDICINE, Manassas,
Virginia, www.vimpva.com/rtran.html

CAROLINE ANIMAL HOSPITAL, Milford, Virginia,
www.carolinevet.com

ALTERNATIVES VETERINARY SERVICE, New Castle,
Virginia, www.alternativesvet.com

BOULEVARD VETERINARY HOSPITAL FOR
INTEGRATIVE HEALING, Norfolk, Virginia, www.blvdvet.com

HILLARY COOK, DVM (ORANGE VETERINARY CLINIC),
Orange, Virginia, www.orangevetclinic.com

PAMPLIN ANIMAL WELLNESS SERVICES, Pamplin, Virginia,
www.wellpaws.com

BETTY BAUGH'S ANIMAL CLINIC, Richmond, Virginia,
www.bettybaughsanimalclinic.com

VETERINARY HOLISTIC AND REHABAILITATION
CENTER, Vienna, Virginia, www.vetrehab.org

Washington

ANIMAL WELLNESS AND REHABILITATION CENTER,
Bellevue, Washington, www.holistic-pet-care.com

ANIMAVET (WHOLISTIC HEALTH AND REHAB FOR
HORSES), Bellevue, Washington, www.animavet.com/animavet.html

MOUNTAIN VETERINARY HOSPITAL, Bellingham, Washington, www.mtnvet.com

WHOLE PET VET (DONNA KELLEHER, DVM), Bellingham, Washington, www.wholepetvet.com

PETSYNERGY HOLISTIC VETERINARY MEDICINE, Brinnon, Washington, www.petsynergy.com

ISSAQUAH VETERINARY HOSPITAL, Issaquah, Washington, www.vetsivh.com

HAWKS PRAIRIE VETERINARY HOSPITAL, Lacey, Washington, www.hawksprairieveterinaryhospital.com

ALL ANIMALS AND BIRD CLINIC, Lake Stevens, Washington, www.holisticanimaldoc.com

ANIMAL HOSPITAL OF LYNNWOOD (TEJINDER SODHI, DVM), Lynnwood, Washington, www.holistic-pet-care.com

HELPING HANDS VETERINARY CLINIC, Lynnwood, Washington, www.helpinghandsvet.com

MERCY VET, Mercer Island, Washington, www.mercyvet.com

EVERGREEN HOLISTIC VETERINARY CARE, Monroe, Washington, www.evergreenholisticvet.com

COLEMAN ANIMAL HEALTH CENTER, Pasco, Washington, www.animalhealing.net

BIG VALLEY VETERINARY SERVICES, Poulsbo, Washington, www.bigvalleyanimalcarecenter.com

ANIMAL HEALING CENTER, Redmond, Washington, www.animalhealingcenter.com

CARKEEK PARK VETERINARY HOSPITAL, Seattle, Washington, www.carkeekparkvh.com

West Virginia

ANIMALIA HOLISTIC VETERINARY CARE, Berkeley Springs, West Virginia, www.animaliaveterinarycare.com

Wisconsin

BURLEIGH ROAD ANIMAL HOSPITAL, Brookfield, Wisconsin, www.burleighroadanimalhospital.com

M & M AROMAPET, Cross Plains, Wisconsin, www.drmaryhess.com

DAIRYLAND VETERINARY CLINIC, Dairyland, Wisconsin, www.dairylandvetclinic.com

NORTHWOODS VETERINARY CENTER Gillett, Wisconsin, www.northwoodsvetcenter.com

COUNTRYCARE ANIMAL COMPLEX, Green Bay, Wisconsin, www.countrycareac.com

HARMONY VETERINARY SERVICES, Madison, Wisconsin, www.harmonyvet.com

HANDS-ON HEALING: A HOLISTIC VETERINARY SERVICE, Milwaukee, Wisconsin, www.handsonhealing4animals.com

ANIMAL DOCTOR HOLISTIC VETERINARY COMPLEX, Muskego, Wisconsin, www.animaldoctormuskego.com

CHRIS BESSENT, DVM, SC (HERBSMITH), Oconomowoc, Wisconsin, www.herbsmithinc.com

HEALING OASIS WELLNESS CENTER, Sturtevant, Wisconsin, www.healingoasis.edu

RISING SUN ANIMAL WELLNESS CENTER, Viroqua, Wisconsin, www.risingsunvet.com

Wyoming

HEALING WAYS VETERINARY CARE, Laramie, Wyoming, (307) 742-2488

Canada

DR. DOBIAS HEALING SOLUTIONS (MY HOLISTIC VET), North Vancouver, British Columbia, www.peterdobias.com

SHUSWAP VETERINARY CLINIC, Salmon Arm, British Columbia, www.shuswapvet.com

FLEETWOOD VETERINARY CLINIC, Surrey, British Columbia, www.fleetwoodveterinaryclinic.com

BRANDON ANIMAL CLINIC (TRACY RADCLIFFE, DVM), Brandon, Manitoba, www.brandonanimalclinic.ca

AESOPS VETERINARY CARE, Winnipeg, Manitoba, www.aesopsvetcare.wordpress.com

NATURAL HEALING VETERINARY CARE, Winnipeg, Manitoba, www.naturalhealingvet.com

FULL CIRCLE VETERINARY ALTERNATIVES, Dartmouth, Nova Scotia, www.fcvetalternatives.com

BURGESS VETERINARY MOBILE SERVICES, Millgrove, Ontario, www.burgessvet.com

NOTTAWASAGA VETERINARY SERVICES, Thornbury, Ontario, www.nottawasagavet.com

EAST YORK ANIMAL CLINIC HOLISTIC CENTRE, Toronto, Ontario, www.holisticpetvet.com

MY TCM VET (VETERINARY ACUPUNCTURE AND TRADITIONAL CHINESE MEDICINE), Toronto, Ontario, www.mytcmvet.com

ATLANTIC VETERINARY COLLEGE, Charlottetown, Prince Edward Island, www.upei.ca/avc/

Index